Better Homes and Gardens®

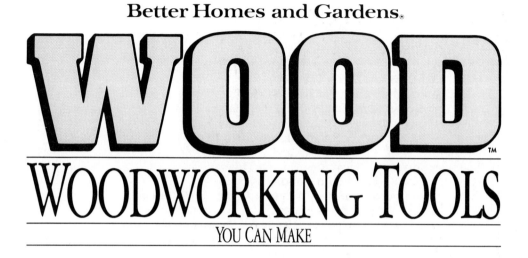

WOOD™
WOODWORKING TOOLS
YOU CAN MAKE

All of us at Meredith® Books are dedicated to giving you the
information and ideas you need to create beautiful and useful
woodworking projects. We guarantee your satisfaction with this
book for as long as you own it. We also welcome your comments
and suggestions. Please write us at Meredith® Books, LS-356WT,
1716 Locust St., Des Moines, IA 50336.

A **WOOD**™ **BOOK**
Published by Meredith® Books

MEREDITH® BOOKS
Vice President, Editorial Director: Elizabeth P. Rice
Art Director: Ernest Shelton
Managing Editor: David A. Kirchner
Project Editors: James D. Blume, Marsha Jahns
Project Managers: Liz Anderson,
    Jennifer Speer Ramundt, Angela K. Renkoski

Associate Art Directors: Neoma Thomas,
    Linda Ford Vermie, Randall Yontz
Assistant Art Directors: Lynda Haupert, Harijs Priekulis,
    Tom Wegner
Graphic Designers: Mary Schlueter Bendgen,
    Michael Burns, Mick Schnepf
Art Production: Director, John Berg; Associate, Joe Heuer;
    Office Manager, Michaela Lester

President, Book Group: James F. Stack
Vice President, Retail Marketing: Jamie L. Martin
Vice President, Administrative Services: Rick Rundall

WOOD® MAGAZINE
President, Magazine Group: James A. Autry
Editorial Director: Doris Eby
Editor: Larry Clayton

MEREDITH CORPORATION OFFICERS
Chairman of the Executive Committee: E. T. Meredith III
Chairman of the Board: Robert A. Burnett
President and Chief Executive Officer: Jack D. Rehm

WOODWORKING TOOLS YOU CAN MAKE
Project Editor: James D. Blume
Contributing Project Editor: James A. Hufnagel
Contributing How-To Editor: Marlen Kemmet
Graphic Designers: Michael Burns, Tom Wegner
Project Manager: Angela K. Renkoski
Contributing Text Editors: Barbara L. Klein, Mary L. Price
Publishing Systems Text Processor: Paula Forest

Special thanks to Kathy Stevens

On the front cover: Benchtop Router Table, pages 38–40
On the back cover (clockwise from top left):
    Handscrew Clamps, pages 5–7; Pocket-Size Try Square,
    pages 8–10; Strip Sander, pages 11–13

Meredith® Books also publishes Better Homes and Gardens® Books,
Country Home™ Books, Meredith® Press Books, and Sedgewood®
Press Books.

HAND TOOLS

*Clamping . . . squaring . . . sanding . . .
scraping . . . marking . . . pounding . . . mitering—
everyday woodworking tasks become even more
satisfying when you accomplish them with hand tools
you've crafted yourself. Here are nine handsome projects
you'll reach for again and again.*

HANDSCREW CLAMPS

If you're like most woodworkers we know, you could use a few more handscrew clamps around your shop. Now you can make your own. Our instructions tell how to build 8″ handscrew clamps (pictured *opposite*). Be sure to see the Buying Guide on page 7 for our source of the hardware for this and the other sizes of clamps available. And, don't forget to order the brass "WOOD Collector's Edition" emblem we've had computer-engraved for this project. It really sets these clamps apart from the rest.

Note: You'll need ½″-thick walnut and maple for the clamp jaws. Either resaw or plane thicker stock to size. (We positioned the tablesaw fence ½″ from the blade and resawed ¾″-thick stock to ½″ thick.)

Machine the jaw parts

1. Cut four pieces of ½″-thick maple and two pieces of ½″-thick walnut to 1¾″ wide by 8″ long.

2. Using double-faced tape, stick together two pieces of maple face-to-face, with the edges and ends flush. Repeat with the two remaining maple pieces and then with the two walnut pieces.

3. Using carbon paper or photocopies and spray adhesive, transfer the full-sized patterns (A, B, C, D) on page 6 to each lamination. Cut the walnut pieces (B, C, D) to shape. *continued*

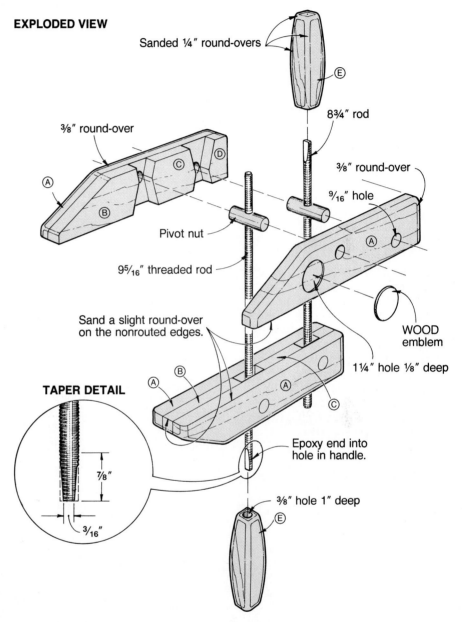

EXPLODED VIEW

Sanded ¼″ round-overs

Ⓔ

8¾″ rod

⅜″ round-over

Ⓐ   Ⓒ   Ⓓ

Ⓑ

⅜″ round-over

9/16″ hole

Pivot nut

Ⓐ

9⁵⁄₁₆″ threaded rod

Sand a slight round-over on the nonrouted edges.

WOOD emblem

Ⓑ

Ⓐ

Ⓐ

Ⓒ

1¼″ hole ⅛″ deep

TAPER DETAIL

7/8″

3/16″

Epoxy end into hole in handle.

⅜″ hole 1″ deep

Ⓔ

HANDSCREW CLAMPS
continued

Laminate the jaws

1. With a $^9/_{16}''$ bit chucked in a drill press, bore two holes through each pair of maple pieces where located on the patterns. (For smooth operation of the pivot nuts in the holes, we recommend a brad-point bit.)

2. Taper the fronts of each maple lamination on a bandsaw. Pry apart all the taped-together pieces, remove the tape, and clean off the sticky residue with lacquer thinner.

3. Using the pivot nuts for alignment and the walnut pieces spaced apart where shown on the Full-Sized Clamp Body Pattern, *right,* glue and clamp together each clamp jaw as shown in photo A, *opposite, left.* (For even clamping pressure, and to prevent denting the maple, we used plywood scraps as clamp blocks. We adhered the plywood to the maple pieces with double-faced tape.) To keep the walnut pieces from sliding around, let the glue get a bit tacky before clamping. Check for slippage after clamping. Remove any excess glue from the openings with a chisel.

4. Later, remove the pivot nuts and scrape off the excess glue. Rout $^3/_8''$ round-overs along the edges of each jaw where shown on the Exploded View Drawing, page 5. Sand smooth.

5. Drill a $1^1/_4''$ hole $^1/_8''$ deep where shown on the full-sized pattern for the engraved "WOOD Collector's Edition" emblem. (We used a Forstner bit, but a spade bit also would work.) For better adhesion, sand the back of the emblem, then epoxy it into the hole.

Add our customized handles, if desired

Note: The kit comes with turned handles. However, our handles give you a firmer grip and look better than the turned ones.

1. Start with a piece of walnut $1^1/_4 \times 1^1/_4 \times 12''$ long. (We laminated $^3/_4''$ stock, then jointed both faces to keep the joint line centered.) Crosscut two pieces $3^3/_4''$ long from the 12" length.

2. Mark diagonals on one end of each $3^3/_4''$-long handle blank (E) to find the center. Drill a $^3/_8''$ hole 1" deep centered in the end of each.

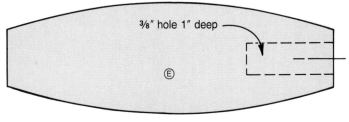

$^3/_8''$ hole 1" deep

Ⓔ

**FULL-SIZED
HANDLE PATTERN**

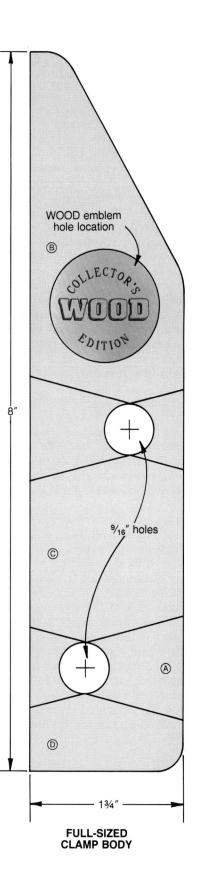

WOOD emblem
hole location

Ⓑ

$^9/_{16}''$ holes

Ⓒ

Ⓐ

Ⓓ

8"

$1^3/_4''$

**FULL-SIZED
CLAMP BODY**

Use a temporary dowel handle for stability when bandsawing the walnut handle to shape.

Brush glue onto the mating surfaces, and clamp the jaw parts together with the edges and ends flush.

3. Stick a 12″ length of ⅜″ dowel into each of the walnut handles to act as a temporary grip.

4. Transfer the Full-Sized Handle Pattern, *opposite,* to one face of each handle blank, and bandsaw along the marked handle lines, as shown in photo B, *above right.* Using double-faced tape, stick the waste pieces back on the edges from which they were cut. Now transfer the handle outline to an adjacent surface and cut it to shape.

5. Still using the dowel handles as grips, use a stationary belt sander to remove the saw marks from the handles. With a palm sander, sand ¼″ round-overs along the edges, then sand the handles smooth.

Apply the finish, and install the clamp hardware kit

1. Remove the dowel handles. Apply an oil finish to each part (we used Watco Natural Oil).

2. Thread the rods through the pivot nuts as described in steps 7, 8, and 9 of the instructions supplied with the clamp hardware. Close the clamps until the jaws are flush against each other. Grind or file the handle end of each threaded rod to the shape shown on the Taper Detail, page 5.

3. Epoxy the handles onto the tapered end of each threaded rod where shown on the Exploded View Drawing, page 5. Immediately wipe off any excess epoxy on the rods.

4. If the handles turn a bit rough, put a drop or two of lubricant (we used WD-40) on each threaded rod. Then, open and close each clamp a few times.

Supplies: double-faced tape, epoxy, spray adhesive or carbon paper, finish.

Buying Guide
• **Handscrew clamp kits.** Each kit contains two threaded rods, four pivot nuts, and two turned handles. Catalog no. P110. Contact Leichtung Workshops, 4944 Commerce Parkway, Cleveland, OH 44128, or call 800-321-6840 or 216/831-6191, for kit prices and shipping charges.

We've provided Leichtung with full-sized patterns for building 6″, 10″, 12″, and 14″ handscrew clamps. The patterns will be included with each clamp hardware kit.
• **Computer-engraved brass emblems.** To order, send $1.04 (U.S.) per emblem along with a self-addressed stamped envelope to Custom Awards, 1427 NW. 81st St., Des Moines, IA 50311.
• ⁹/₁₆″ **brad-point bit.** Carbon steel with ½″ shank. Catalog no. 200-½. For current price, contact Puckett Electric Tools, 841 Eleventh St., Des Moines, IA 50309, or call 800-544-4189 or 515/244-4189.

POCKET-SIZE TRY SQUARE

There are few tools more indispensable in a workshop than an accurate square. That's why we're so pleased to be able to share this tried-and-true project design with you. Are the squares accurate? You bet they are. Several of us on the *WOOD*® magazine staff spent a few hours in the shop constructing seven squares using the drawings and instructions shown here. Then we sent our squares to the College of Technology at Bowling Green State University in Ohio for testing. All of the squares measured to within .008" of perfect square—well within the requirements of home woodworkers.

Begin with the walnut body

1. Cut a piece of ¾" walnut to ¾" wide by 7¾" long. (We searched through our walnut stock until we found a piece with highly figured grain. Also, we cut the piece extra long for safety when routing the coves in the next step.) If you rout coves on both ends before crosscutting, you'll have enough stock for two handles.

2. Chuck a ⅜" core-box bit into a table-mounted router. Raise the bit ³/₃₂" above the table surface where shown on the End Section Detail, *opposite.* Position the fence exactly ⅜" from the center of the bit.

3. Clamp two stops to your router table fence where shown in the Cove Routing Setup Drawing, *opposite.* With one end of the walnut against Stop 1, lower the face-grain edge onto the bit and push the walnut to Stop 2 to rout the groove. Repeat the procedure on the opposite surface of the walnut.

4. Crosscut the routed end of the walnut to 3¼" long.

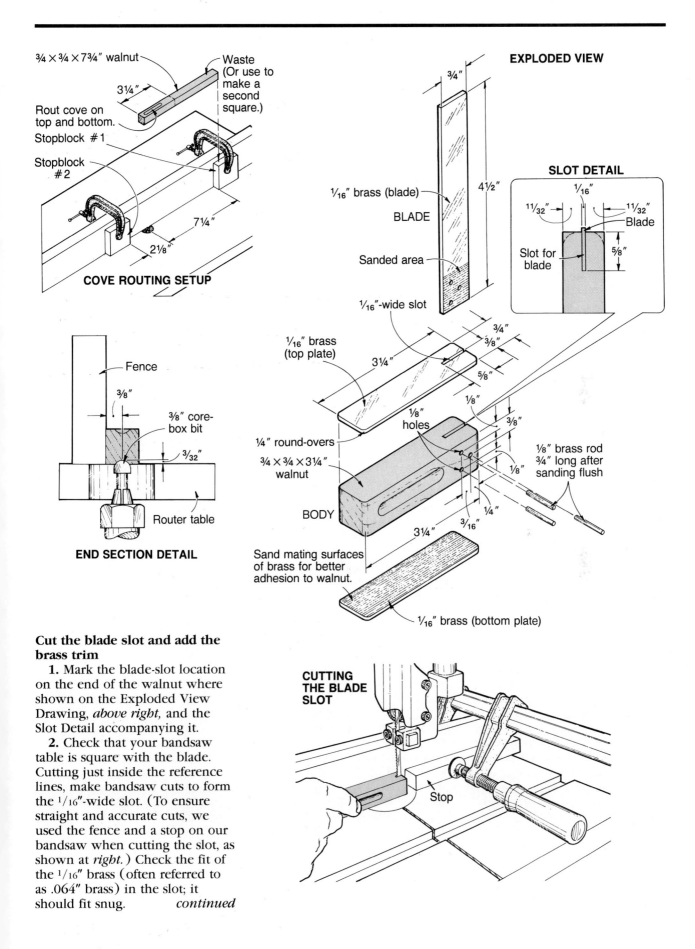

¾ × ¾ × 7¾" walnut

Waste (Or use to make a second square.)

Rout cove on top and bottom.

Stopblock #1

Stopblock #2

3¼"

7¼"

2⅛"

COVE ROUTING SETUP

Fence

⅜"

⅜" core-box bit

3/32"

Router table

END SECTION DETAIL

EXPLODED VIEW

¾"

4½"

1/16" brass (blade)

BLADE

Sanded area

1/16"-wide slot

SLOT DETAIL

1/16"

11/32"

11/32"

Blade

Slot for blade

5/8"

1/16" brass (top plate)

3¼"

¾"

⅜"

5/8"

1/16" brass

⅛" holes

⅛"

⅜"

⅛"

¼" round-overs

¾ × ¾ × 3¼" walnut

BODY

3¼"

3/16"

¼"

⅛" brass rod ¾" long after sanding flush

Sand mating surfaces of brass for better adhesion to walnut.

3¼"

1/16" brass (bottom plate)

Cut the blade slot and add the brass trim

1. Mark the blade-slot location on the end of the walnut where shown on the Exploded View Drawing, *above right,* and the Slot Detail accompanying it.

2. Check that your bandsaw table is square with the blade. Cutting just inside the reference lines, make bandsaw cuts to form the 1/16"-wide slot. (To ensure straight and accurate cuts, we used the fence and a stop on our bandsaw when cutting the slot, as shown at *right.*) Check the fit of the 1/16" brass (often referred to as .064" brass) in the slot; it should fit snug. *continued*

CUTTING THE BLADE SLOT

Stop

POCKET-SIZE TRY SQUARE
continued

3. Cut two pieces of $1/16 \times 3/4''$ brass to 3¼″ long each (the same length as your walnut handle) from one 12″ length of brass for the top and bottom plates. See the Buying Guide for our source of brass.

4. For better adhesion with the quick-set epoxy, sand one surface of each brass piece with 80-grit sandpaper. With the edges and ends flush, epoxy and tape (we used masking tape) one of the brass pieces (the top plate) to the walnut. Then, with the brass side down, use the previously cut slot in the walnut to bandsaw the same-sized slot in the brass.

5. Being careful not to get any epoxy inside the slot, epoxy the other piece of brass (the bottom plate) to the opposite surface.

6. File and sand the edges of the brass and walnut flush. (We used a file to round the edges, and then sanded the body on a stationary sander.) Be careful not to let the brass get hot; otherwise, the epoxy will soften, causing the brass to delaminate from the walnut.

7. Sand or file a slight round-over on each corner of the square body. (We used a disc sander.)

Install the blade accurately

Note: To position the blade as square as possible to the handle, we found it much better to start with a 12″ brass blade and trim it to length after epoxying and pinning it in place.

1. Cut a piece of particleboard to 13″ wide by about 10″ long. Joint one edge of the particleboard.

2. Sand the bottom ¾″ of a 12″ length of brass for better adhesion. Using a toothpick, spread some quick-set epoxy into the slot in the body.

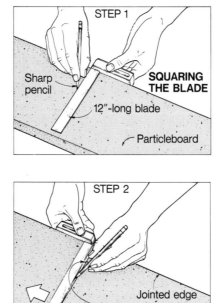

3. Slide the blade into the slot. Immediately wipe off excess epoxy. Before the epoxy hardens (in less than 5 minutes), use an existing square to position the blade at a 90° angle to the body. Being careful not to jar the blade out of alignment, position the square's body against the jointed edge of the particleboard. Mark a line, the length of the blade, across the board (see the Step 1 Drawing, *top*). Use a sharpened pencil; the sharper the lead, the more accurately you can position the blade. Flop the square as shown in the Step 2 Drawing, *above,* and mark a second line. Repeat the process, adjusting the blade until the lines align perfectly. Let the epoxy cure. If after the epoxy cures, your blade is not square with the body, file the blade with a mill bastard file, following the Step 1 and Step 2 drawings to check for square.

4. With an awl, mark indentations for the brass-rod holes where dimensioned on the Exploded View Drawing, page 9. With a twist-drill bit, drill three ⅛″ holes through the body and blade. Cut three pieces of ⅛″ brass rod ⅞″ long. Epoxy a brass rod in each hole. File and sand the ends of the rods flush with the edges of the walnut as shown in the photo *below.*

File the ends of the brass rods flush with the surface of the walnut.

5. Crosscut the blade to 4½″ long. (We supported ours on an $^{11}/_{32}''$-thick block of wood and trimmed it to length on the bandsaw.)

6. Sand the walnut with 220- and 320-grit sandpaper. Polish the brass with 600-grit paper or brass polish. Finish the brass and walnut with an aerosol lacquer.

Buying Guide
● **Brass.** Two pieces of $1/16 \times 3/4 \times 12''$ brass, ⅛″ brass rod 6″ long. Catalog no. 100PS. 8″ mill bastard file also available. For current prices, contact Puckett Electric Tools, 841 Eleventh St., Des Moines, IA 50309, or call 800-544-4189 or 515/244-4189.

STRIP SANDER

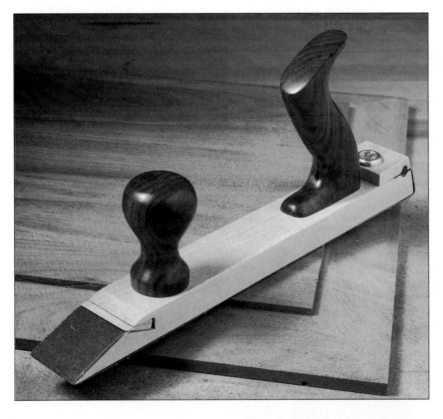

If you're a stickler for details (and every woodworker should be!), we hope you build this terrific walnut and maple strip sander. "It's the perfect tool for cleaning cabinet joinery," says Jim Downing, our design editor. We agree. With this tool, you can sand right up to an edge or corner for the smoothest surfaces imaginable.

Start with the maple body

1. Rip and crosscut a piece of ¾"-thick maple to 1½" wide by 13½" long for the strip-sander body (A).

2. Using the two dimensions marked in the Step 1 Drawing, *below, far left,* mark an angled cutline on one edge of the maple body. Cut along the marked line. (We used our bandsaw fitted with a ⅜" blade.)

3. Following the Step 2 Drawing, *bottom left,* cut the wedge (B) from the waste piece of maple.

4. Mark a reference line along either side of the maple body 3/16" from the top edge where shown on the Step 2 Drawing. Position the maple wedge along this line as shown in photo A, *center left,* and trace its outline onto the side of the maple body. Cut the notch to shape, and check the fit of the wedge in the slot; you want it to slide in easily.

5. Sand a round-over on the front edge of the maple body and wedge (see the Step 2 Drawing again for reference). Sand the body smooth.

Fashion the hold-down

1. Bandsaw the abrasive strip hold-down (C) (see the Exploded View Drawing on page 12) to ⅜" thick by 1½" wide by 1¹¹/₁₆" long. (We cut a ¾"-thick piece of maple to 1½" wide by 12" long—you need the extra length for safety. Then we planed the stock to ⅜" thick and crosscut the hold-down to length from the strip.) *continued*

Mark the reference line, position the wedge along the line, and trace the wedge outline onto the side of the body.

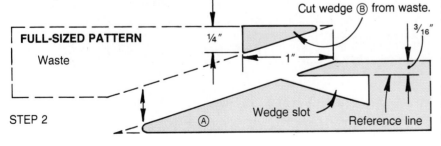

10⅛"

12½"

STEP 1

FULL-SIZED PATTERN

Waste

STEP 2

¼"

1"

Cut wedge Ⓑ from waste.

³⁄₁₆"

Ⓐ

Wedge slot

Reference line

STRIP SANDER
continued

EXPLODED VIEW

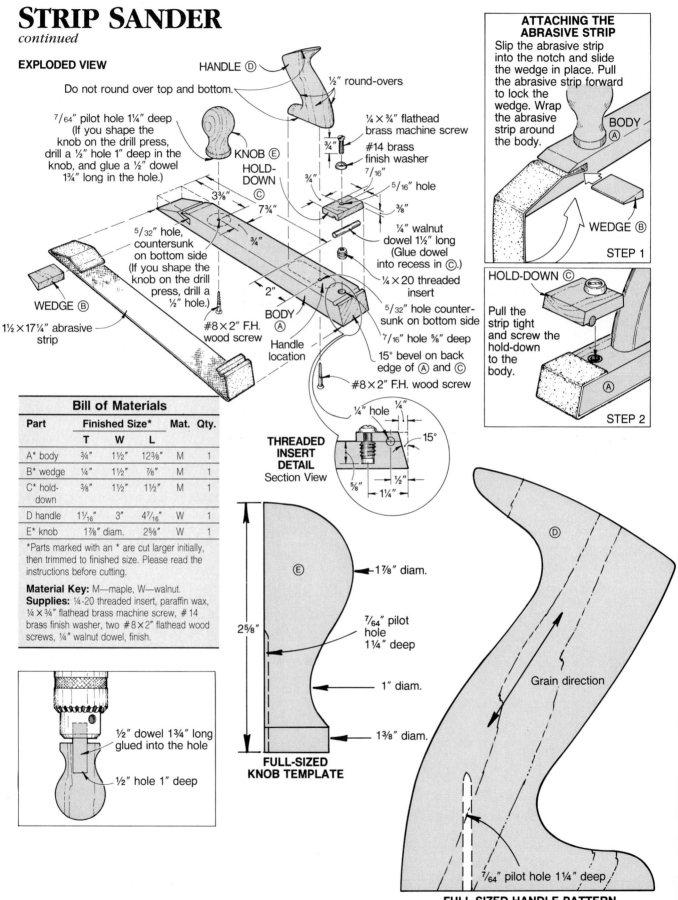

HANDLE Ⓓ
½" round-overs

Do not round over top and bottom.

⁷/₆₄" pilot hole 1¼" deep
(If you shape the
knob on the drill press,
drill a ½" hole 1" deep in the
knob, and glue a ½" dowel
1¾" long in the hole.)

KNOB Ⓔ

HOLD-
DOWN
Ⓒ

¼ × ¾" flathead
brass machine screw
¾"
#14 brass
finish washer
⁷/₁₆"

3⅜"
7¾"
⁵/₃₂" hole,
countersunk
on bottom side
(If you shape the
knob on the drill
press, drill a
½" hole.)

¾"
¾"

⁵/₁₆" hole
⅜"

¼" walnut
dowel 1½" long
(Glue dowel
into recess in Ⓒ.)

¼ × 20 threaded
insert

⁵/₃₂" hole counter-
sunk on bottom side

⁷/₁₆" hole ⅝" deep

15° bevel on back
edge of Ⓐ and Ⓒ

WEDGE Ⓑ

1½ × 17¼" abrasive
strip

2"

#8 × 2" F.H.
wood screw

BODY
Ⓐ

Handle
location

#8 × 2" F.H. wood screw

ATTACHING THE ABRASIVE STRIP
Slip the abrasive strip
into the notch and slide
the wedge in place. Pull
the abrasive strip forward
to lock the
wedge. Wrap
the abrasive
strip around
the body.

BODY
Ⓐ

WEDGE Ⓑ

STEP 1

HOLD-DOWN Ⓒ
Pull the
strip tight
and screw the
hold-down
to the
body.

Ⓐ

STEP 2

**THREADED
INSERT
DETAIL**
Section View

¼" hole
¼"
15°
½"
⁵/₈"
1¼"

Bill of Materials

Part	Finished Size*			Mat.	Qty.
	T	W	L		
A* body	¾"	1½"	12⅜"	M	1
B* wedge	¼"	1½"	⅞"	M	1
C* hold-down	⅜"	1½"	1½"	M	1
D handle	1¹/₁₆"	3"	4⁷/₁₆"	W	1
E* knob	1⅞" diam.		2⅝"	W	1

*Parts marked with an * are cut larger initially,
then trimmed to finished size. Please read the
instructions before cutting.

Material Key: M—maple, W—walnut.
Supplies: ¼-20 threaded insert, paraffin wax,
¼ × ¾" flathead brass machine screw, # 14
brass finish washer, two #8 × 2" flathead wood
screws, ¼" walnut dowel, finish.

½" dowel 1¾" long
glued into the hole

½" hole 1" deep

**FULL-SIZED
KNOB TEMPLATE**

Ⓔ

1⅞" diam.

⁷/₆₄" pilot
hole
1¼" deep

1" diam.

1⅜" diam.

2⅝"

Ⓓ

Grain direction

⁷/₆₄" pilot hole 1¼" deep

FULL-SIZED HANDLE PATTERN

2. Measure ⁷/₁₆″ from the front end of the hold-down, and mark the hole centerpoint for the brass machine screw where dimensioned on the Exploded View Drawing, *opposite*. Secure the hold-down in a small handscrew clamp, and drill a ⁵/₁₆″ hole through it where marked.

3. Position the hold-down on the body, with the back and side edges flush. Trace the hole location onto the body, remove the hold-down, and drill a ⁷/₁₆″ hole ⅝″ deep centered over the drawn circle.

4. Rub the threads of a ¼-20 threaded insert against a piece of paraffin wax (this makes driving the insert into the maple easier). Using a large screwdriver, drive the insert into the ⁷/₁₆″ hole in the body. With a ¼ × ¾″ machine screw and #14 finish washer, screw the hold-down to the body.

5. Mark the centerpoint for the ¼″ dowel on the joint line between the body and the hold-down (see the Threaded Insert Detail, *opposite, center,* for exact location). As shown in photo B, *below,* drill a ¼″ hole on the joint line where marked.

Mark the centerpoint on the joint line, then drill a ¼″ hole where marked.

6. Mark the angled cutline along the back side edge of the body and hold-down (again, see the detail). Miter-cut the body and hold-down where marked. Remove the hold-down from the body.

7. From ¼″ walnut dowel stock, cut a piece 1½″ long. Glue and clamp the dowel into the groove drilled into the hold-down.

Make the handle

1. Using carbon paper, transfer the handle pattern to 1¹/₁₆″ walnut, noting the direction of the grain on the Full-Sized Handle Pattern, *opposite.* If you don't have 1¹/₁₆″ walnut, laminate thinner stock to size.

2. Bandsaw the handle to shape. With your table-mounted router, rout ½″ round-overs along the edges. *Do not* rout the top and bottom of the handle. (We stopped routing just short of the top and bottom. Then we sanded to the top and bottom edges to complete the round-overs.)

3. To mount the handle, first refer to the Exploded View Drawing, *opposite,* for the position of the ⁵/₃₂″ mounting hole, then mark its centerpoint. Drill and countersink the hole.

4. Carefully position the handle on the body (see the Exploded View Drawing again). Stick a nail up through the hole in the body to mark the centerpoint on the bottom of the handle. Drill a ⁷/₆₄″ pilot hole 1¼″ deep in the bottom of the handle. Sand the handle smooth and set it aside.

Turn the knob to shape

1. To make the knob (E), begin with a 2″ square piece of walnut 3″ long. If you don't have stock this thick, laminate thinner stock.

2. Using carbon paper, transfer the Full-Sized Knob Template Pattern, *opposite,* to poster board. Cut the template to shape.

3. Mount the walnut square between centers on the lathe. Turn the knob to shape, using the template. Finish-sand the knob before removing it from the lathe.

Note: If you don't have a lathe, you can drill a ½″ hole 1″ deep, centered on the bottom of the knob blank. Glue a ½″ dowel 1¾″ long in the hole. Using a rasp and the template, shape the knob on your drill press as shown opposite, bottom left. To mount the handle, drill a ½″ hole through the body at the same location where you'd drill the hole for the #8x2″ wood screw.

4. Referring to the Exploded View Drawing for positioning particulars, locate and then drill a ⁵/₃₂″ shank hole through the body (A); countersink the hole on the bottom side.

5. Hold the knob in a handscrew clamp, and drill a ⁷/₆₄″ pilot hole 1¼″ deep into the center of it.

Add the finish and the sanding strip

1. Glue and screw the handle and knob to the body. Screw the hold-down in place. Add the finish.

2. Cut a 17¼″-long piece from a 1½″-wide abrasive roll (see the Buying Guide for our source; you also could cut sanding belts to make the strip). To attach the abrasive strip to the body, follow the two steps in the drawings, *opposite, top right.*

Buying Guide
• **Cloth-backed abrasive shop roll.** 1½″ wide by 25 yards long. Available in 60-, 80-, 100-, 120-, 150-, 180-, 240-, 320-, and 400-grit rolls. Catalog no. 101AR; please specify grit desired. For current prices, contact Puckett Electric Tools, 841 Eleventh St., Des Moines, IA 50309, or call 800-544-4189 or 515/244-4189.

FINE-FINISH SCRAPER

Here's a scraper that's as comfortable as it is good-looking. The adjustable blade makes getting into tight corners a snap.

Make the handle

1. Cut a ½"-thick piece of walnut to 2½" wide by 17" long for the handle parts (A, B). (We resawed a piece of ¾" walnut to ½" thick; you also could plane or joint a thicker piece to ½".) Cut the 17" walnut strip in half.

2. Cut or rout a ¼" groove ¼" deep down the center of part A where shown on the Side View Detail, *opposite*. (We used a dado blade on the tablesaw to cut the groove.)

3. Using a dado blade on either the tablesaw or radial-arm saw, cut a 1¼" rabbet ³/₃₂" deep across the grooved face of the handle bottom (A).

4. Tilt your saw blade 40° from vertical, and bevel-cut the front end of each handle part.

5. Glue and clamp the handle pieces together with the edges flush. Align the mitered ends where shown on the Side View Detail.

6. Enlarge the Handle Pattern, *opposite*. Using spray adhesive, attach the pattern onto the bottom face of the walnut handle lamination. Bandsaw the handle to shape. Drum-sand the contours smooth to remove the saw marks.

7. Chuck a ⅜" round-over bit into your table-mounted router. Rout the handle where shown on

A

Secure the all-thread rod in a vise or handscrew clamp, and file a ¼" notch ⅛" deep ½" from the end.

B

Scribe marks every 2½" on the hacksaw blade. Then, shear scraper blades to length with a cold chisel.

C

Angle the scraper slightly less than 45°. Using straight strokes, file the blade with a mill bastard file.

the Exploded View Drawing, *right*. Sand a ½″ round-over on the front top end of the handle where shown on the same drawing. Sand the handle smooth and apply the finish.

Shape, then add the hardware

1. Apply masking tape to the polished side (the top face) of a solid-brass door strike. (See the Buying Guide for our hardware kit.) The tape is easy to mark cutlines on and helps prevent the polished brass from being marred when cutting.

2. Mark a centerline across the strike where shown on the Door Strike Drawing, *below, near right*. Using the drawing dimensions, trim the strike ends and front lip. File burrs from the cut edges.

3. Clamp ⅞″ of the strike in a vise and bend the exposed portion as shown on the Bending the Strike Drawing, *far right*. Place the strike in the handle to check the angle; continue bending until the angle is the same as the front of the handle. (See the Side View Detail accompanying the Exploded View Drawing for reference.)

4. Cut a 7½″ length of ¼″ all-thread rod. As shown in photo A, *opposite,* use a #8 mill bastard file to cut a notch in the threaded rod. See the Notch Detail, *top right,* for dimensions. (We wrapped masking tape around the rod to mark the notch location on the rod and to prevent marring the rod threads in the vise.)

5. To make the scraper blades, mark increments every 2½″ on a used or dull hacksaw blade. Clamp the blade in a vise. Using a cold chisel, shear off the blade segments where marked, as shown in photo B, *opposite.* Hammer the corners of each blade flat—they tend to bend slightly when chiseling to length.

6. Assemble the scraper, and slip the scraper blade into position. Tighten the wing nut on the all-thread rod to hold the scraper blade in position. (We kept ⅛″ of the blade exposed.)

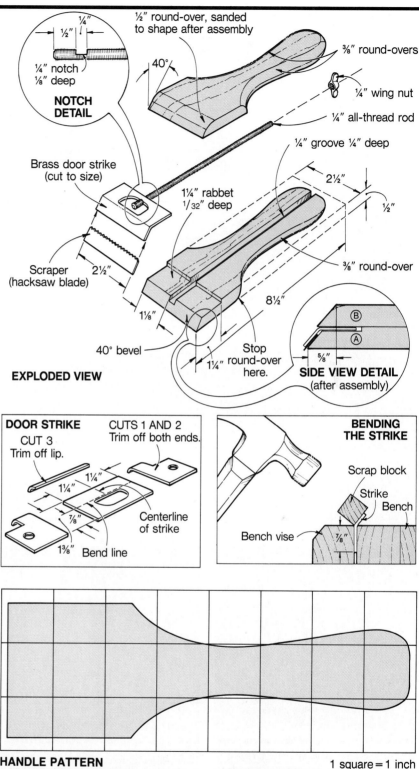

EXPLODED VIEW

NOTCH DETAIL

DOOR STRIKE
CUT 3 — Trim off lip.
CUTS 1 AND 2 — Trim off both ends.
Centerline of strike
Bend line

BENDING THE STRIKE

HANDLE PATTERN

1 square = 1 inch

Sharpening the blade

To sharpen the blade, angle the scraper as shown in photo C, *opposite,* and sharpen with a mill bastard file. As you move the file back and forth, keep it in contact with the total length of the blade. (We held our scraper at slightly less than 45° when sharpening.)

Buying Guide

• **Scraper hardware kit.** Brass strike plate, ¼″ brass wing nut, ¼″ all-thread rod 7½″ long. Catalog no. 102S. For the current price, contact Puckett Electric Tools, 841 Eleventh St., Des Moines, IA 50309, or call 800-544-4189 or 515/244-4189.

DEPTH GAUGE

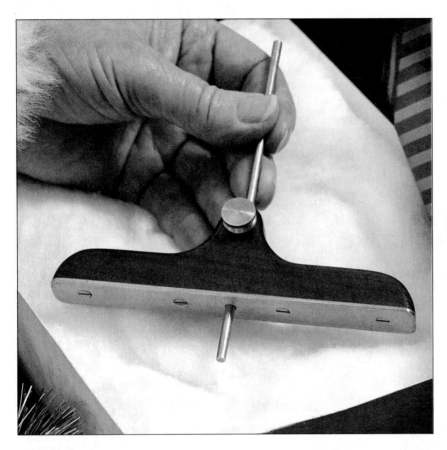

A

Hold the cap in a small handscrew clamp or vise, and file the nipple threads for easy insertion into the walnut body.

B

Center a **5/32"** bit over the walnut, and drill through the walnut and the brass nipple.

You're not likely to misplace this shop heirloom. You may even want to build several of these simple, yet elegant, depth gauges; they make excellent gifts. Used for measuring dadoes, mortises, and other recesses where an exact reading is critical, this is one high-quality measuring tool.

Form the walnut body

1. Cut a piece of ¾"-thick walnut stock to 1¾ × 6" for the body.

2. Make a photocopy of the Full-Sized Pattern, *opposite.* Using spray adhesive, adhere the paper pattern to the walnut. (You could transfer the pattern directly to the walnut with carbon paper.)

3. Mark a centerpoint on the top edge of the walnut directly above and aligned with the ⅜" hole centerpoint. (See photo B, *below, near left,* for reference.)

4. Drill a ⅜" hole ⅝" deep into the face of the walnut at the marked centerpoint.

5. Thread the ⅜" cap onto the ⅜" nipple as far as it will thread. (See the Buying Guide for our hardware source.) As shown in photo A, *far left,* clamp the cap into a handscrew clamp, and file the exposed nipple threads. (We used a dowel to hold the nipple stationary when filing.) File the threads until the nipple slides easily into the hole in the walnut.

6. Hold the nipple (cap still threaded on) with a pair of pliers, and rotate the cap two turns counterclockwise. Push the nipple and cap into the ⅜" hole in the walnut. Drill a ⁵/₃₂" hole through the assembly as shown in photo B.

7. Remove the nipple and cap from the walnut body. Do not remove the paper pattern.

Add the brass base

1. Crosscut a piece of ¹/₁₆ × ¾" brass to 6" long.

2. Use double-faced tape to adhere brass to the bottom of the body. Using the screw-hole location lines on the pattern, drill and countersink $7/64''$ holes through the brass. Switch bits and drill $5/64''$ pilot holes $5/16''$ deep into the walnut. (We held the walnut firmly in a handscrew clamp when drilling the holes.)

Assemble the gauge

1. Remove the brass strip and nipple assembly from the walnut. Bandsaw the walnut body to shape, and sand the cut edges smooth. Rout a $1/4''$ round-over along the top edges. To keep your fingers safely away from the router bit, hold the walnut body firmly in a handscrew clamp. You'll have to stop, reposition the clamp, and continue routing. Remove the remaining paper pattern.

2. Screw the brass strip to the bottom of the walnut. File and sand the edges of the brass strip even with the round-over edges of the walnut. Using the previously drilled $5/32''$ hole in the walnut body as a guide, drill a $5/32''$ hole through the brass for the rod.

3. Sand the depth gauge smooth. Mask the brass and apply the finish to the walnut. Cut a piece of $1/8''$ brass rod to $6''$ long.

Buying Guide

• **Depth-gauge kit.** $3/8''$ brass cap, $3/8''$ nipple $11/16''$ long, $1/16 \times 3/4 \times 6''$ brass strip, $1/8''$ brass rod $6''$ long, 5—#4 $\times 3/8''$ F.H. brass wood screws. Catalog no. 103DG. For the current price, contact Puckett Electric Tools, 841 Eleventh St., Des Moines, IA 50309, or call 800-544-4189 or 515/244-4189.

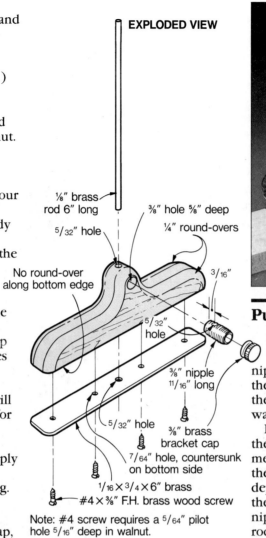

EXPLODED VIEW

$1/8''$ brass rod 6" long
$5/32''$ hole
No round-over along bottom edge
$3/8''$ hole $5/8''$ deep
$1/4''$ round-overs
$3/16''$
$5/32''$ hole
$3/8''$ nipple $11/16''$ long
$5/32''$ hole
$3/8''$ brass bracket cap
$7/64''$ hole, countersunk on bottom side
$1/16 \times 3/4 \times 6''$ brass
#4 $\times 3/8''$ F.H. brass wood screw

Note: #4 screw requires a $5/64''$ pilot hole $5/16''$ deep in walnut.

Putting the Depth Gauge to Work

Thread the cap onto the nipple, and insert the nipple into the walnut. Align the $5/32''$ hole in the nipple with the hole in the walnut. Insert the $1/8''$ brass rod.

Position the depth gauge over the depression you wish to measure, as shown *above*. Push the brass rod to the bottom of the depression. Tighten the cap on the nipple. The cap will pull the nipple forward and lock the brass rod in place. Measure the length of brass rod protruding from the bottom of the gauge to determine the depth.

Note: If you do a lot of turning, you may want to make a larger version for checking the depth of bowls. To do so, increase the length of the walnut body, brass strip, and brass rod.

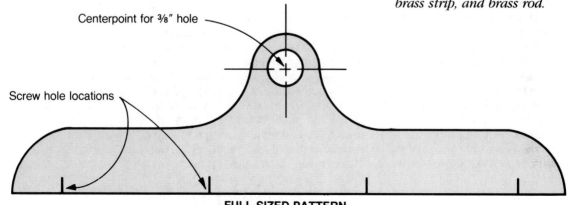

Centerpoint for $3/8''$ hole

Screw hole locations

FULL-SIZED PATTERN

SANDING BLOCK

This idea comes from *WOOD*® magazine subscriber M. C. "Morrie" Patten of Mesa, Arizona, who makes his laminations long enough to yield at least two sanding blocks at a time. That way they're easier to machine, and he has several to give to his woodworking buddies. We were so impressed with Morrie's blocks, we decided to make a couple for our shop and share his idea with you.

Make the sanding block bases

1. Rip and crosscut a piece of ¾″ maple to 2¼ × 10″ long, enough for two bases (A). Then joint, resaw, or hand-plane the maple to ⅝″ thickness.

2. Rip two strips of walnut ¼″ wide from the edge of a piece of ¾″ stock. Crosscut each to 10″ for the sides (B).

3. Glue and clamp one walnut strip to each edge of the maple, with the *bottom* edges flush. Scrape off any glue squeeze-out.

4. Crosscut two 4½″-long bases from the lamination.

Fashion the palm grips

1. Start by cutting one piece of ¾″ maple (C) and one piece of ¾″ walnut (D) to 2¼ × 10″ long. Using a bandsaw or tablesaw, resaw the walnut into two pieces just under ⅜″ thick each.

2. Glue and clamp the maple between the two pieces of walnut, sandwich-fashion, making sure that all edges align exactly.

3. Remove the clamps and scrape off any excess glue. Then joint or plane the walnut top and bottom pieces to a finished thickness of ¼″ each. Then joint or plane the edges until the palm grip fits snugly between the protruding walnut sides of the base (you'll sand the palm grip to finished width later).

4. Crosscut the palm-grip lamination into two 4½″ lengths.

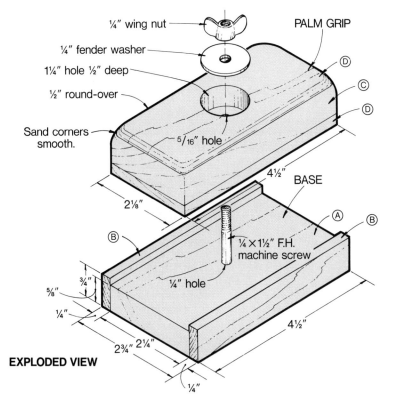

¼″ wing nut
¼″ fender washer
1¼″ hole ½″ deep
½″ round-over
Sand corners smooth.
PALM GRIP
D
C
D
5/16″ hole
4½″
2⅛″
BASE
A
B
B
¼ × 1½″ F.H. machine screw
¼″ hole
¾″
⅝″
¼″
2¾″ 2¼″
4½″
¼″

EXPLODED VIEW

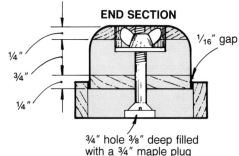

END SECTION

¼″
¾″
¼″
1/16″ gap
¾″ hole ⅜″ deep filled with a ¾″ maple plug

Bill of Materials

Part	Finished Size*			Mat.	Qty.
	T	W	L		
For One Sanding Block					
A* base	⅝″	2¼″	4½″	M	1
B* side	¾″	¼″	4½″	W	2
C* grip	¾″	2⅛″	4½″	M	1
D* grip	¼″	2⅛″	4½″	W	2

*Parts marked with an * are cut larger initially, then trimmed to finished size. Please read the instructions before cutting.

Material Key: M—maple, W—walnut.
Supplies: ¼ x 1½″ flathead machine screw with fender washer and wing nut, epoxy, felt (optional), finish.

Drill the bolt and wing-nut holes

1. Mark diagonals on the top of each palm grip to locate its center; position the palm grip in the base with the ends flush. Clamp the palm grip and base to your drill-press table, and drill a ⅛″ guide hole through both pieces as shown in the photo, *bottom left*. (For this and the following steps, we machined both sanding-block pieces at once.)

2. Separate the two pieces, and, using a flat-bottomed bit, drill a 1¼″ hole ½″ deep into the *top* of the palm grip, centered over the guide hole (see the End Section Drawing, *above right,* for hole-size details). Then drill and counterbore a ¾″ hole ⅜″ deep centered over the guide hole on the *bottom* side of the base.

3. Drill a ¼″ hole through the base and a 5/16″ hole through the palm grip, centering both holes on the guide hole. Countersink the ¼″ hole on the *bottom* side of the base.

4. Hand-plane or sand 1/16″ off each side (not the ends) of the palm grip for a 2⅛″ finished width.

5. Clamp the base, bottom up, in a woodworker's vise. Thread a ¼ × 1½″ machine screw through the hole and tighten the palm grip to the base with a wing nut. Epoxy the screw in the hole in the base. Cut a ¾″ maple plug, and epoxy it over the head of the screw.

6. Detach the base from the palm grip, and sand the plug flush with the base. Sand the base smooth.

7. Fit your table-mounted router with a ½″ round-over bit, and rout the top edges of the palm grip. Finally, sand the palm grip to fit comfortably in your hand.

8. You may want to cut and glue a piece of felt to the bottom of one or all of the sanding blocks for sanding pieces with slight contours. Trim the edges of the felt flush with the base.

Assemble and finish

1. Fit a fender washer in the hole in the palm grip. Then apply the finish of your choice to the base and palm grip.

2. To use, slip the palm grip over the bolt on the base, and just start the wing nut. Quarter a standard sheet of sandpaper, and tuck the sides under the palm grip. Tighten the wing nut to hold the sandpaper firmly in position.

MARKING GAUGE

This brass-bound beauty will make its mark on your projects for many years to come.

Note: You'll need thin stock for this project. You can either plane or resaw thicker stock to size. See the Buying Guide for our source of hardware to make the marking gauge.

Start with the body

1. Cut a ½"-thick piece of walnut to 1" wide by 12" long. (We resawed ¾" stock.) Cut two pieces 2¾" long for body parts A and two pieces to 1" long for body parts B from the 12" piece.

2. Rip a 4" length of ¾" scrap lumber to ½" wide for the temporary spacer, as shown *below.* Sand ¹⁄₁₆" from one side

BODY LAMINATION

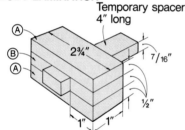

Temporary spacer 4" long

and surface of the spacer and then rub a coat of wax onto the spacer so it won't bond to the body parts during glue-up. With the edges and ends flush, glue and clamp the body parts together. Remove the spacer after the pieces are firmly clamped together.

3. Cut or rout ¼" dadoes ¹⁄₁₆" deep in the body lamination where shown *above right* to accommodate the brass. (Brass is available at most hobby shops that carry model-building supplies. If you have trouble locating it, see the Buying Guide for our source.)

HOLE AND DADO LOCATION

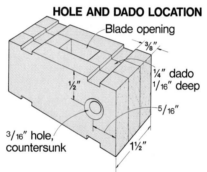

Blade opening
³⁄₈"
¼" dado ¹⁄₁₆" deep
½"
⁵⁄₁₆"
³⁄₁₆" hole, countersunk
1½"

4. Drill and countersink a ³⁄₁₆" hole through the body lamination where shown on the drawing *above.* Check the fit of a 10-24×2" brass machine screw in the hole. The surface of the screw head should be flush with the surface of the lamination.

5. Clamp the body in a woodworker's vise, and use a fine-toothed blade (we used a dovetail saw) to cut a slot through the end of the body where shown on the Exploded View Drawing, *opposite.*

6. Crosscut the brass strips to size indicated on the Exploded View Drawing. Fit the brass into the dadoes, and drill and countersink the mounting holes to the sizes listed on the Exploded View Drawing. Epoxy and screw the brass strips into the dadoes; immediately wipe off any

excess epoxy. Next install the tightening bolt, using epoxy in the countersink to prevent movement of the bolt.

7. File any excess brass protruding from the ends of the dadoes. Sand the body smooth.

Add the blade

1. Cut two pieces of ½"-thick maple to ⁵⁄₁₆" wide by 8" long for blade parts (C). From ½"-thick walnut stock, cut the blade center (D) to ³⁄₈" wide by 7" long. (Part D is cut extra wide for safety in trimming in the next step.)

2. Glue and clamp the walnut strip to one of the maple strips, holding the walnut back 1" from the end of the maple to create a slot for the lead/scribe holder. After the glue dries, rip the walnut to ³⁄₃₂" wide, as shown *below.* Then glue and clamp the remaining maple strip to the glued-up blade assembly.

RIPPING THE HANDLE CENTERPIECE

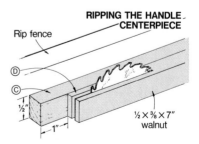

Rip fence
D
C
½"
1"
½ × ³⁄₈ × 7" walnut

3. Sand the blade as necessary so it will pass through the opening in the body lamination. Then drill and countersink the hole in the notched end of the blade to accept the blade-tightening bolt (see the Exploded View Drawing). Epoxy the head of the bolt in the countersink. Thread the knurled nut onto the bolt to apply some pressure, but not so much that the slot is reduced to less than 1/32". Drill a 1/16" hole into the blade to accept a lead or scribe.

4. Cut 3/4" rabbets 1/16" deep in the opposite end of the blade to accept the brass plates. Cut the brass plates to size, and epoxy them in place. After the epoxy dries, file the brass smooth and sand the blade smooth.

Form the lead/scribe storage hole, and add the finish

1. Mark the center of the blade's end, and fit the marked end into the opening of the body, shown at *right*. Clamp the body to the drill-press table as shown. Snug the tightening bolt so the blade won't move in the body.

2. Slowly drill a 3/8" hole 1 1/4" deep centered into the marked end of the blade. Switch bits, and drill a 3/16" hole 1/4" deep in the center of the 3/8" hole.

3. Cut the head off a 10-24×2" brass machine screw so the threaded portion measures 1 3/4" long. Place a small amount of epoxy onto the end of the threaded rod, and screw it into the 3/16" hole, until 1/4" of the rod protrudes from the end of the blade for the knurled nut. Store your leads or metal scribe in the cavity (3/8" hole) around the threaded rod.

4. Lightly sand the parts smooth, and add the finish.

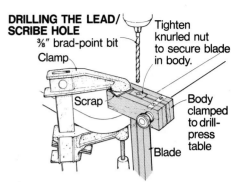

DRILLING THE LEAD/SCRIBE HOLE
3/8" brad-point bit
Clamp
Tighten knurled nut to secure blade in body.
Scrap
Body clamped to drill-press table
Blade

Buying Guide
• **Marking-gauge hardware kit.** 2—1/16×1/4×3 1/4" brass strips, 1—1/16×3/4×3 1/4" brass strip (1/16"-thick brass is commonly called .064 brass in hobby shops), 3—10-24×2" F.H. brass machine screws, 3—10-24 brass knurled nuts, 8—#4×1/2" F.H. brass screws, metal scribe. Catalog no. 104MG. For the current price, contact Puckett Electric Tools, 841 Eleventh St., Des Moines, IA 50309, or call 800-544-4189 or 515/244-4189.

Bill of Materials					
Part	Finished Size*			Mat.	Qty.
	T	W	L		
A* body side	1/2"	1"	2 3/4"	W	2
B* body center	1/2"	1"	1"	W	2
C blade side	1/2"	5/16"	8"	M	2
D* blade center	1/2"	3/32"	7"	W	1

*Parts marked with an * are cut larger initially, then trimmed to finished size. Please read the instructions before cutting.

Material Key: W—walnut, M—maple.
Supplies: epoxy, wax, finish, plus kit listed in the Buying Guide.

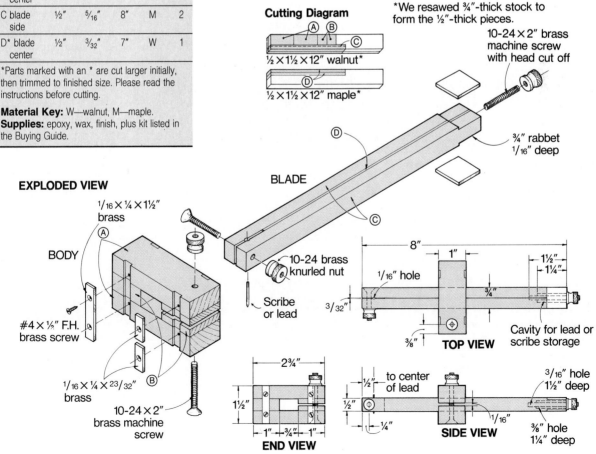

Cutting Diagram
*We resawed 3/4"-thick stock to form the 1/2"-thick pieces.
1/2×1 1/2×12" walnut*
1/2×1 1/2×12" maple*

10-24×2" brass machine screw with head cut off

3/4" rabbet 1/16" deep

BLADE

EXPLODED VIEW
1/16×1/4×1 1/2" brass
BODY
#4×1/2" F.H. brass screw
1/16×1/4×23/32" brass
10-24×2" brass machine screw
10-24 brass knurled nut
Scribe or lead

TOP VIEW
8"
1"
1 1/2"
1 1/4"
1/16" hole
3/4"
3/32"
3/8"
Cavity for lead or scribe storage

END VIEW
2 3/4"
1 1/2"
1" 3/4" 1"

SIDE VIEW
1/2"
1/2"
to center of lead
1/4"
1/16"
3/16" hole 1 1/2" deep
3/8" hole 1 1/4" deep

HARD MAPLE WOODWORKER'S MALLETS

It's no accident that skilled woodworkers everywhere count a wooden mallet as one of their most trusted tools. It has dozens of uses—from nudging home a tight-fitting joint to driving a chisel.

Both of our custom mallets feature large leather-protected striking surfaces that dampen and diffuse contact over a large area. We show you how to fashion the version with the octagon-shaped head using a tablesaw and a few hand tools. The other style, a design alternative if you like lathe work, closely resembles the first in construction. If you choose the variation, refer to the Lathe-Turned Mallet Drawing, *below*, as your guide.

Note: You'll need thick stock for the mallet heads and handles. You can either laminate thinner stock to size or purchase turning squares. For the leather striking surfaces, we bought leather rounders from a local Tandy outlet.

1. Rip the mallet head (A) to $2\frac{3}{4} \times 2\frac{3}{4}''$ and crosscut it to length. Find and mark the centerpoint of one of its edge-

LATHE-TURNED MALLET

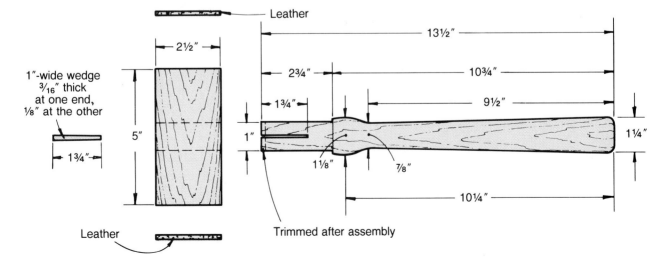

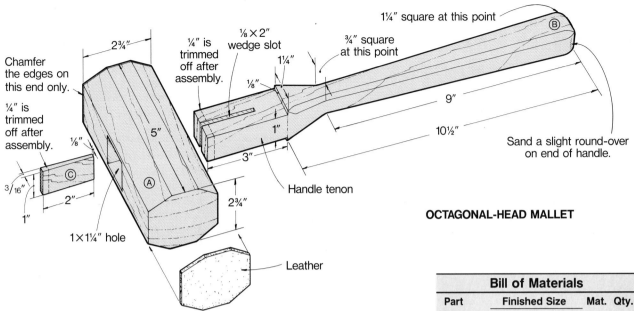

2¾"

Chamfer the edges on this end only.

¼" is trimmed off after assembly.

⅛"

³⁄₁₆"

1"

2"

© C

1 × 1¼" hole

© A

5"

¼" is trimmed off after assembly.

⅛ × 2" wedge slot

⅛"

1¼"

¾" square at this point

1¼" square at this point

© B

1"

3"

Handle tenon

2¾"

2¾"

Leather

9"

10½"

Sand a slight round-over on end of handle.

OCTAGONAL-HEAD MALLET

Bill of Materials					
Part	Finished Size			Mat.	Qty.
	T	W	L		
A head	2¾"	2¾"	5"	M	1
B handle	1¼"	1¼"	13½"	M	1
C wedge	³⁄₁₆"	1"	2"	M	1

Material Key: M—maple.
Supplies: epoxy, tung oil, paste wax, leather.

grain sides. Using a 1" spade bit, bore a hole into the head at the centerpoint, stopping when the point of the bit just protrudes through the opposite side to prevent chip-out. Turn the piece over and finish boring the hole.

2. Carefully chisel the hole in the mallet head to form a 1¼ × 1" rectangle, working from both sides to avoid chip-out.

3. To transform the square stock into the octagonal shape, first tilt the blade on your table-saw to 45° and set the fence 2¹⁵⁄₁₆" away from the base of the blade where shown in the drawing *below*. Then, using a pushstick, feed the stock along the fence and bevel-rip the edges.

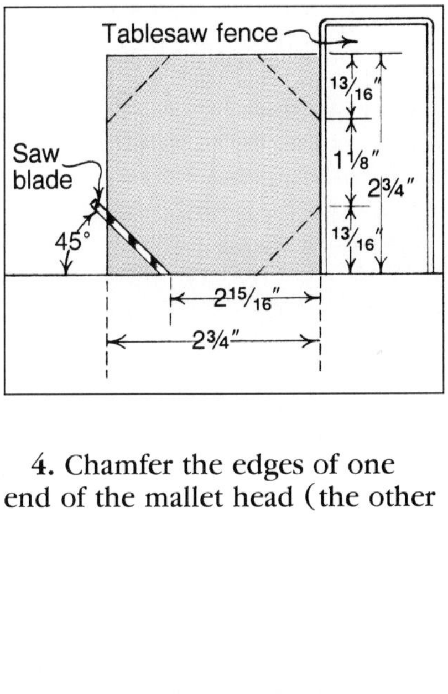

Tablesaw fence

Saw blade

45°

13⁄16"

1⅛"

2¾"

13⁄16"

2¹⁵⁄₁₆"

2¾"

4. Chamfer the edges of one end of the mallet head (the other

end will be covered with leather and should not be chamfered).

5. Rip and crosscut the handle (B) to size. Cut a pair of ⅛" deep recesses 3" long to form the handle tenon as shown in the Octagonal-Head Mallet Drawing, *above*. (We used a tablesaw, miter gauge, and a dado blade to make the pair of recess cuts.) Make sure the handle tenon fits snugly in the hole in the mallet head. With a bandsaw or jigsaw, cut the handle to shape as indicated on the drawing. Then use a spokeshave or scraper to make bevel cuts on the edges of the handle as shown in the photo, *below*.

6. With a fine-toothed handsaw or a bandsaw, cut a ⅛" slot 2" long to house the tenon wedge in the recessed end of the handle.

7. Fashion a wedge (C) from scrap maple. Then spread glue on the tenon and in the hole in the mallet head, and insert the handle into the hole. Now run a few beads of glue into the slot in the handle, cover the wedge with glue, and tap the wedge snugly into position. (This will be the last time you'll have to use a hammer for this type of operation!) Remove the excess glue, and, after the glue dries, carefully saw off the excess material protruding through the head.

8. Finish-sand the entire mallet. Then epoxy and clamp the leather in place *opposite* the chamfered end. When the epoxy cures, trim the leather flush with the edges of the head with a crafts knife. Finish the mallet (not the leather) with tung oil followed by a couple of applications of paste wax.

WALNUT-MAPLE MITER BOX

By making the critical cuts on the tablesaw before assembly, you guarantee that this homemade miter box will deliver power-tool accuracy whenever you hand-cut the smallest of parts.

Note: Your miter box will be only as accurate as the saw cuts you make. Cut scrap stock and check each of the angles before starting. Also, keep the distance between the front and back fence at exactly 3".

Cut the pieces

1. Cut the maple front fence (A) and back fence (B) to the sizes listed in the Bill of Materials plus 1" in length, making sure the crosscuts are square. Cut the base (C) to size, and cut two pieces of ¾" walnut to 2" wide by 11" long for D and E.

2. Measure and mark the position of the six dovetail grooves on the front and back fences. Using a tablesaw and a ⅛" blade, cut a kerf down the center of the marked dovetail grooves (see photo A, *below, far left*). This removes most of the wood needed to form the dovetail grooves. (We found that routing a dovetail groove without first cutting the kerfs can make the router bit wander or burn the wood.)

3. Fit your table-mounted router with a ¹³/₃₂" dovetail bit. (We used one from Sears.) Attach a fence and feather board to the router table as shown in photo A. With the top of the bit ⅜" above the table surface, cut the dovetail grooves in both fences (A, B), making one pass through the previously cut saw kerfs.

4. Reposition the fence, but not the cutting height of the bit. Cut tongues in center of edges of C as shown in photo B, *left;* then rout

A

B

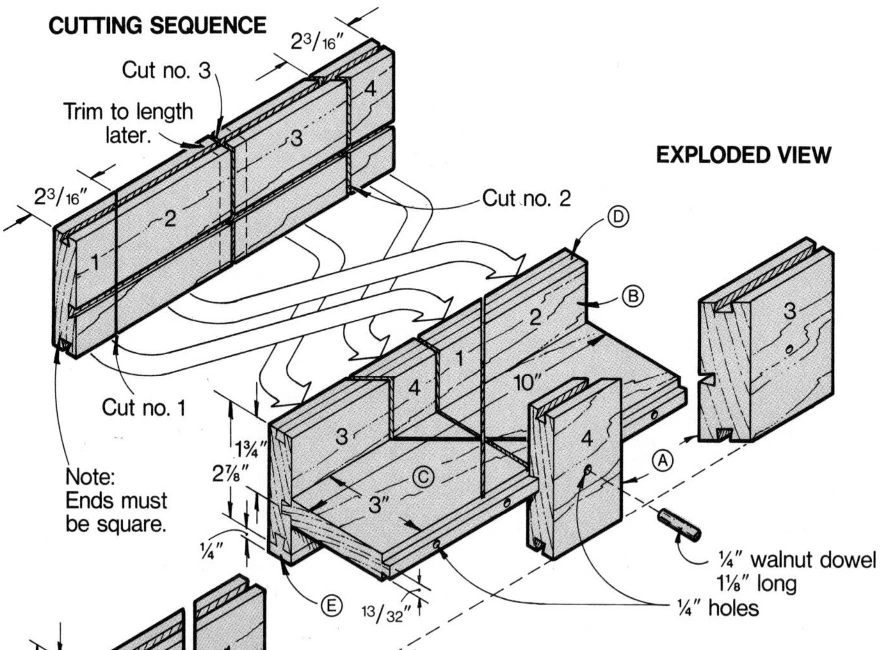
CUTTING SEQUENCE
2³/₁₆″
Cut no. 3
Trim to length later.
2³/₁₆″
Cut no. 2
Cut no. 1
Note:
Ends must be square.
EXPLODED VIEW
1¾″
2⅞″
3″
10″
¼″
13/32″
¼″ walnut dowel 1⅛″ long
¼″ holes

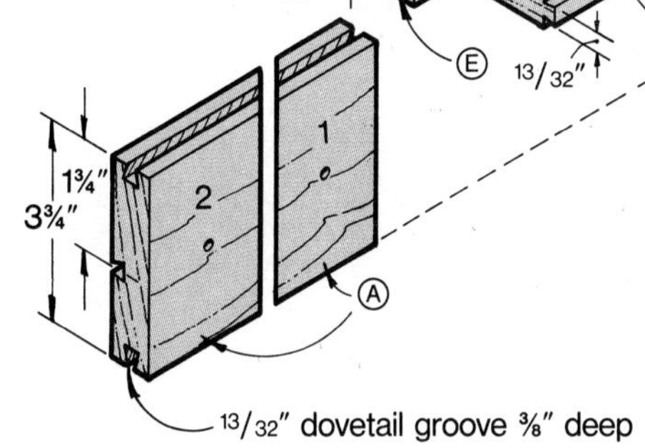
1¾″
3¾″
13/32″ dovetail groove ⅜″ deep

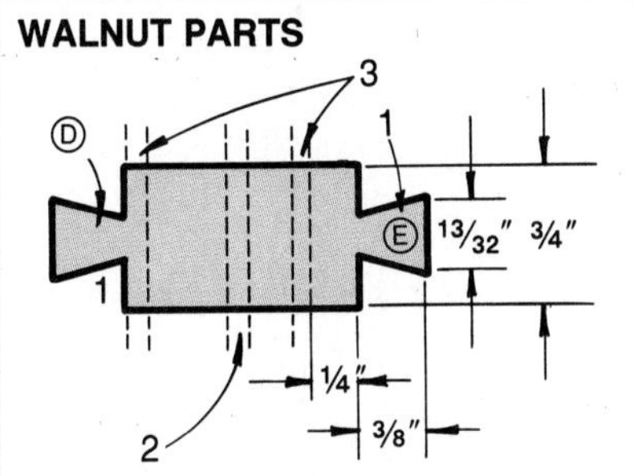
WALNUT PARTS
13/32″
¾″
¼″
⅜″

1 Cut tongues first.
2 Cut in half to separate D and E.
3 Cut after inserting in fence grooves.

Bill of Materials

Part	Finished Size* T	W	L	Mat.	Qty.
A* front fence	¾″	3¾″	10″	M	1
B* back fence	¾″	2⅞″	10″	M	1
C base	¾″	3¾″	10″	M	1
D* strip	13/32″	⅜″	10″	W	2
E* strip	¾″	⅝″	10″	W	2

*Parts marked with an * are cut larger initially, then trimmed to finished size. Please read the instructions before cutting.

Material Key: M—maple, W—walnut.
Supplies: ¼″-diameter walnut dowel stock, polyurethane.

the edges of the walnut blanks for strips D and E where shown in the Walnut Parts Drawing, *above.* (We cut the tongues slightly oversize at first, and moved the fence closer to the bit until the tongues fit snugly.)

Cut the fence into sections

1. Using a stop block, make miter cuts no. 1 and no. 2 on each end of both fences (A, B) where shown in the Cutting Sequence portion of the Exploded View Drawing, *above.* To facilitate positioning later, mark numbers in pencil on the maple sections where shown.

2. Make cut no. 3 in the center of each fence to form sections no. 2 and no. 3.

Assemble the miter box

1. Mark a line at 90° across the center of the base (C). Glue and slide sections no. 1 and no. 4 of both fences onto the tongues of C. Line up the sections with the marked centerline on C. When positioning, use the blade of the handsaw you will place in the miter box as a spacer between sections no. 1 and no. 4. Check for square against C, and secure sections no. 1 and no. 4 with clamps.

2. Slide (but do not glue) sections no. 2 and no. 3 onto the tongues of C, again using the saw blade as a spacer. Mark the ends of sections no. 2 and no. 3 against the finished length of C (sections no. 2 and no. 3 are still cut long at this point). Slide sections no. 2 and no. 3 off, and trim to length. Now glue and clamp sections no. 2 and no. 3 into position on each fence, again using the blade of the saw as a spacer and checking for square.

3. Rip parts D and E in half to obtain four long pieces, each with a tongue where shown in the Walnut Parts Drawing, *left.* Glue and slide parts D and E into the dovetail grooves in the front and back fences.

4. To further secure the sections in position, drill a ¼″ hole 1″ deep in each section of A and B (eight total holes) into the center of the edges of C. Cut eight pieces of ¼″ walnut dowel stock to 1⅛″ lengths; then glue and drive the dowels into the holes. After the glue dries, trim and sand the dowels flush.

5. Trim off the excess from the ends of the walnut strips (D, E). Now, using the fence on your tablesaw, trim the protruding top edges of D and E to finished size, where dimensioned in the Walnut Parts Drawing.

6. With the same handsaw used earlier, cut through the walnut into the previously cut kerfs in both fences. Finish-sand the miter box and apply two coats of polyurethane.

POWER TOOLS
AND ACCESSORIES

Looking to improve the accuracy and capacity of your tablesaw? Want to table-mount a router, or machine accurate box joints? You'll find lots of ways to boost the performance of your power tools on the pages that follow. We even show you how to build your own lathe and thickness sander.

EASY-TO-ADJUST RIP FENCE

If you're looking for an inexpensive way to upgrade your tablesaw, you've turned to the right pages. After using accurate aftermarket fences, we challenged WOOD® magazine design editor, Jim Downing, to come up with a wooden replacement fence for woodworkers who like to build their own workshop tools and save a bundle of money in the process. Less than 12 hours later, Jim emerged from his workshop, proudly hugging his prototype. We think Jim's design (pictured *opposite*) will please you, too.

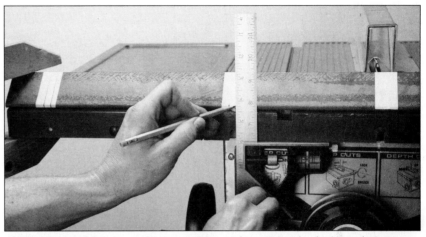

Clamp the angle iron to the saw table, and transfer the hole and slot locations from the saw table to the angle iron.

Note: We designed our replacement rip fence to fit a Sears 10″ motorized tablesaw. Some dimensions may vary for different tablesaws.

Begin with the front rail

1. From ¾″ birch, rip and crosscut three pieces 1¾″ wide by 53″ long for the replacement guide rail (A). With the edges and ends flush, glue and clamp the pieces face-to-face.

2. Later, remove the clamps and scrape off the excess glue.

3. Remove the existing front rail from your tablesaw.

4. Using a hacksaw, cut a piece of 2×2″ angle iron to 53″ long.

5. With the left end of the angle iron flush with the left end of the tablesaw extension, clamp the angle iron to the saw table as shown in photo *above right*.

6. Apply masking tape to the angle iron directly above each bolt hole and slot. Using a square, transfer the tablesaw hole and slot locations onto the tape as shown in the photo. Remove the iron.

7. Drill and countersink ¼″ holes through the angle iron, centering each hole between the

lines and ⅝″ from the top edge of the angle iron. See the Angle Iron Detail on page 28 for reference.

8. Clean the angle iron with paint thinner, sand it smooth, and spray it with rust-resistant black paint.

9. For your fence system to perform correctly when completed, position the top edge of the guide rail (A) ¾″ below the top surface of the saw table. To achieve this with our guide rail, we cut a ¾″ rabbet ¼″ deep along one edge of the rail where shown on the Guide Rail Drawing and accompanying Angle Iron Detail (both on page 28). Your rabbet depth may vary to achieve the ¾″ spacing.

10. Clamp the angle iron to the rabbeted recess where shown on the Angle Iron Detail. Then drill seven additional ¼″ holes through the angle iron where shown on the Guide Rail Drawing. Switch bits and drill ³⁄₁₆″ pilot holes 1¼″ deep into the guide rail.

11. Using ¼×1½″ hex-head lag screws and flat washers, fasten the angle iron to the guide rail.

12. With ¼×1″ flathead machine screws, fasten the angle iron to the saw table, using two ¼″ washers as spacers (see the Angle Iron Detail). Check that the guide rail is parallel with the saw table.

Cut and laminate the fence pieces

1. Cut three pieces of ¾″ plywood (we used birch plywood) to 2½×32″ for the fence parts (B).

2. With carbon paper or a photocopy, transfer the cutlines from the Full-Sized Mechanism Opening Pattern on page 30 to the left end of one plywood strip.

3. Bandsaw along both cutlines to cut the pieces.

4. Position the support block on one of the remaining fence pieces where dimensioned on the pattern. With the bottom edges flush, glue and clamp the support block to the outer fence part where shown on the pattern. Glue and clamp the remaining inner fence part to the same

continued

EASY-TO-ADJUST RIP FENCE

continued

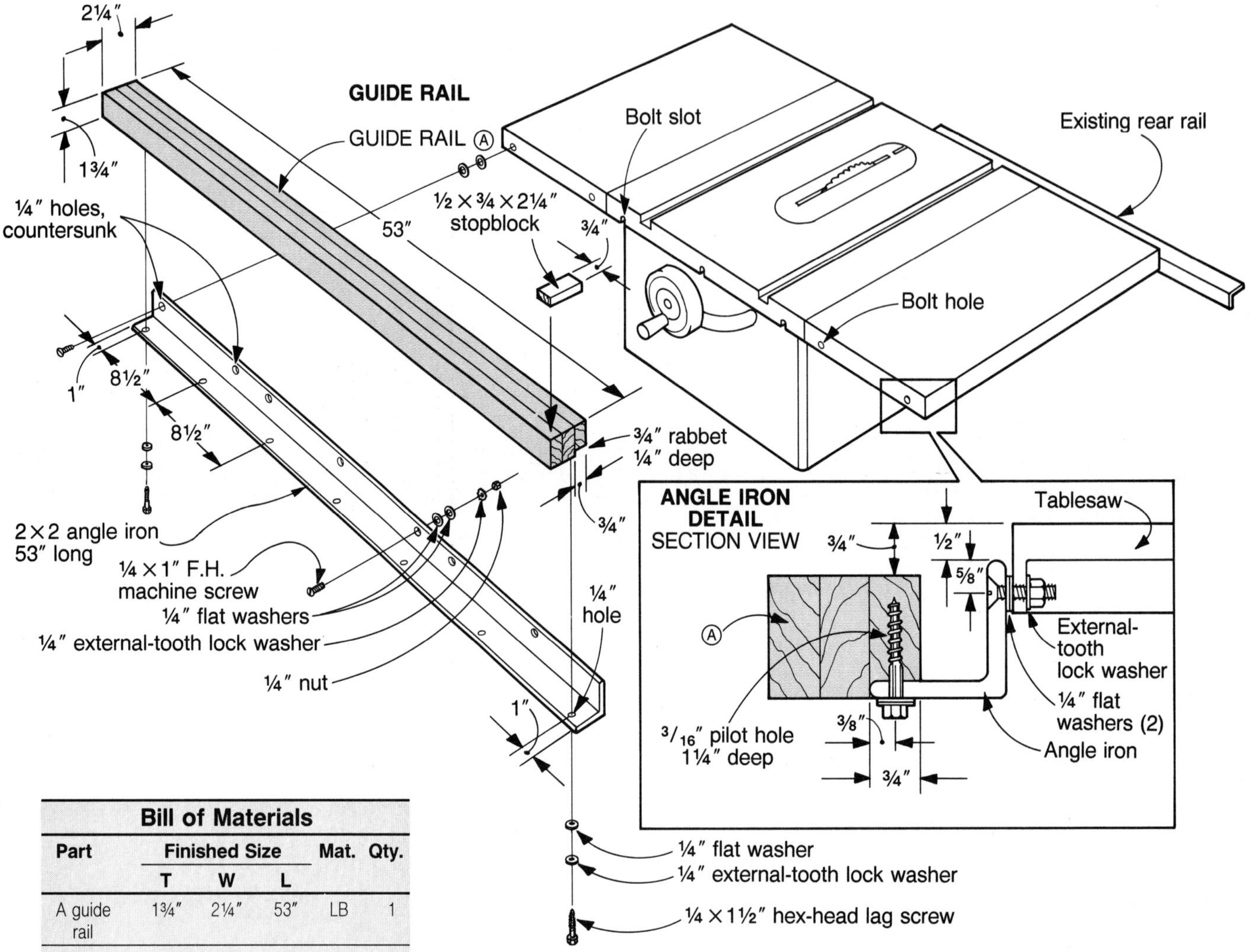
2¼″
1¾″
¼″ holes, countersunk
GUIDE RAIL
GUIDE RAIL Ⓐ
53″
½ × ¾ × 2¼″ stopblock
¾″
Bolt slot
Existing rear rail
Bolt hole
1″
8½″
8½″
¾″ rabbet ¼″ deep
¾″
2×2 angle iron 53″ long
¼ × 1″ F.H. machine screw
¼″ flat washers
¼″ external-tooth lock washer
¼″ nut
¼″ hole
1″
ANGLE IRON DETAIL
SECTION VIEW
¾″
½″
⅝″
Tablesaw
Ⓐ
External-tooth lock washer
¼″ flat washers (2)
Angle iron
3/16″ pilot hole 1¼″ deep
⅜″
¾″
¼″ flat washer
¼″ external-tooth lock washer
¼ × 1½″ hex-head lag screw

Bill of Materials

Part	Finished Size T	W	L	Mat.	Qty.
A guide rail	1¾″	2¼″	53″	LB	1
B fence	¾″	2½″	32″	PLY	3
C locking lever	¾″	1½″	4¼″	B	1
D connecting block	¾″	½″	5⅛″	B	1
E finger clamp	¾″	1 1/16″	3¾″	B	1
F head block	¾″	6¼″	13¾″	PLY	1
G aligning block	1 1/16″	2¼″	13¾″	B	1

Material Key: LB—laminated birch, PLY—plywood, B—birch.
Supplies: ¼ × 2 × 2″ angle iron 53″ long, masking tape, paint thinner, rust-resistant black spray paint, 7—¼ × 1″ flathead machine screws, 23—¼″ flat washers, 14—external-tooth lock washers, 9—¼″ nuts, 7—¼ × 1½″ hex-head lag screws, 2—¼ × 1½″ hex-head machine screws, ¼ × 2″ hex-head machine screw and lock nut, 2—¼″ threaded inserts, ⅜″ dowel stock, 4 each—1½″ and 2½″ drywall (case-hardened) screws, finish.

Cutting Diagram

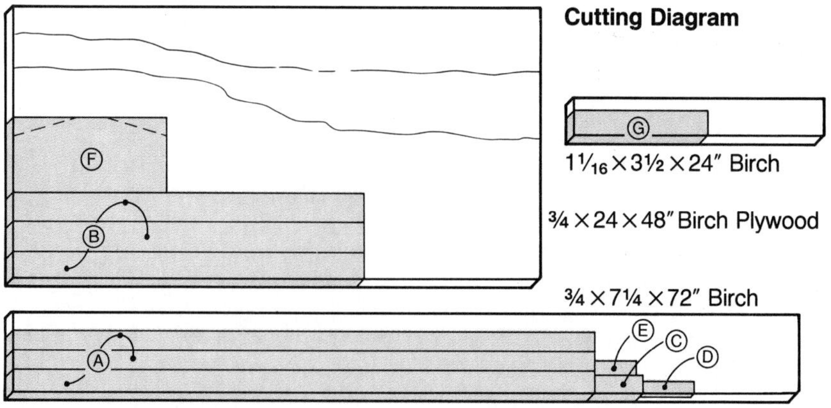
Ⓕ
Ⓑ
Ⓖ
1 1/16 × 3½ × 24″ Birch
¾ × 24 × 48″ Birch Plywood
¾ × 7¼ × 72″ Birch
Ⓐ
Ⓔ
Ⓒ
Ⓓ

outer fence part where shown on the pattern. Remove any excess glue from the opening.

5. With the edges and ends flush, glue and clamp the remaining fence part to the assembly. Be careful not to get any glue in the cutout area. Later, sand a ¼″ round-over along the top front edge where shown on the Fence Drawing, *opposite.*

6. Drill a ¼″ hole through the fence assembly where dimensioned on the Fence Drawing. Now bore a ¾″ hole ¼″ deep and centered over the ¼″ hole on both faces of the fence rail (we used a Forstner bit).

Make the locking mechanism

1. Transfer the full-sized patterns and hole centerpoint for the locking lever (C), connecting block (D), and finger clamp (E) (see page 30) to ¾″ solid birch with carbon paper or by adhering a photocopy to the stock. Bandsaw the pieces to shape. Mark an X on the lever where shown.

2. Drill a ¼″ hole through the locking lever where marked. Slide the connecting block in place and bolt the lever in position. Locate the edge with the X next to the connecting block where shown on the Fence Drawing. To keep the lever moving freely, don't overtighten the nut on the machine screw. Slide the finger clamp in place.

Construct the fence-head assembly

1. Using the Head Block Drawing, *middle right,* for reference, mark the outline, notch, and the eight centerpoints for the head block (F) on ¾″ plywood. Bandsaw the head block to shape and sand smooth.

2. For mounting the fence to the head block later, drill four ⅛″ holes where shown on the Head Block Drawing. Then drill four ⁷⁄₆₄″ holes through the head block at the remaining marked centerpoints.

3. Cut the aligning block (G) to size. Using the Aligning Block Drawing, *bottom right,* for reference, transfer the ⅛″ hole centerpoints and kerf locations to the block. Drill the two ⅛″ holes where marked. Now position your bandsaw fence 2″ from the blade. Starting at one end of the block, cut to the ⅛″ hole. Stop the saw, and back the piece away from the blade. Switch ends, and cut to the other ⅛″ hole as

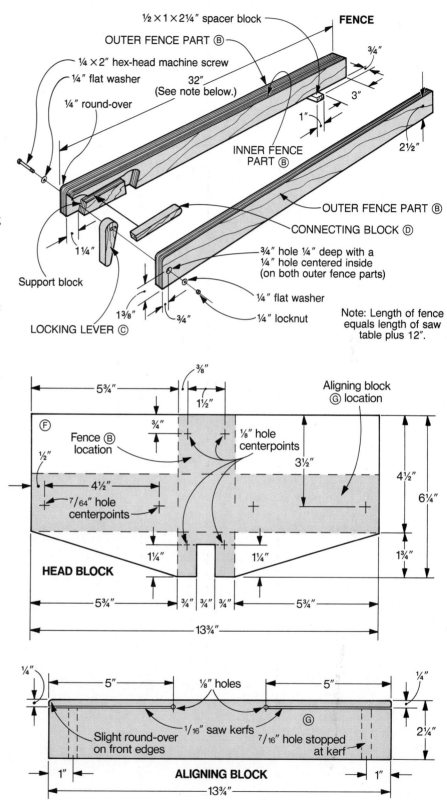

shown in photo A, page 30. Sand a slight round-over on the front edges of the block where shown on the Fence Drawing.

4. Position the aligning block on edge with the kerfed edge on your workbench. On the opposite edge, mark the *continued*

EASY-TO-ADJUST RIP FENCE
continued

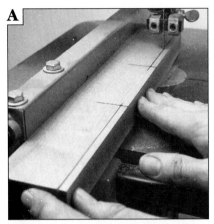

A

Position the bandsaw fence and align the blade with the center of the ⅛" holes in the aligning block. Bandsaw to the holes to form a pair of kerfs in the aligning block.

⁷⁄₁₆" hole locations for the threaded inserts where shown on the Aligning Block Drawing. Drill ⁷⁄₁₆" holes 2" deep, centered from edge to edge (stop drilling when you reach the bandsawed kerf).

5. Cut two pieces of ⅜" dowel 1¼" long, and slide one into each ⁷⁄₁₆" hole in the aligning block. Wax the threads of two ¼" threaded inserts, and screw the

inserts into the ⁷⁄₁₆" holes in the aligning block. Thread a ¼" nut on each of the two ¼×1½" hex-head screws. Thread a screw into each insert.

6. Position and clamp the aligning block to the bottom side of the head block. (See the Head Block Drawing, page 29, for location.) Using the previously drilled ⁷⁄₆₄" holes as guides, drill ⁷⁄₆₄" holes ¾" deep into the

aligning block. Screw (no glue yet) the aligning block to the bottom side of the head block.

7. Position and clamp the fence head (F, G) to the bottom side of the locking end of the fence (B), *carefully* checking for square. Using the previously drilled ⅛" holes in the head block as guides, drill ⅛" holes 1¾" deep into the bottom of the fence. Screw the assemblies together as shown in photo B, *opposite*.

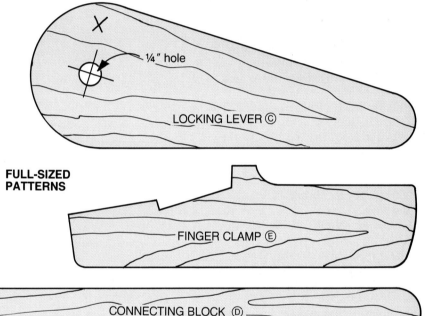

X

¼" hole

LOCKING LEVER Ⓒ

FULL-SIZED PATTERNS

FINGER CLAMP Ⓔ

CONNECTING BLOCK Ⓓ

FULL-SIZED MECHANISM OPENING

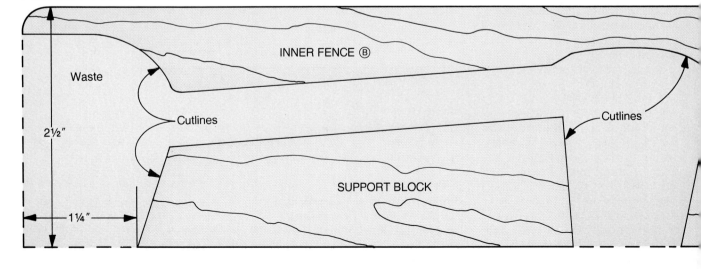

INNER FENCE Ⓑ

Waste

Cutlines

Cutlines

2½"

1¼"

SUPPORT BLOCK

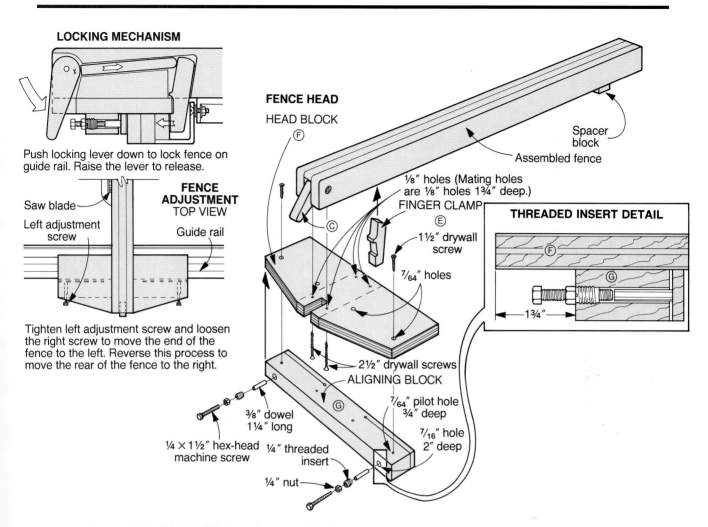

LOCKING MECHANISM

Push locking lever down to lock fence on guide rail. Raise the lever to release.

FENCE ADJUSTMENT
TOP VIEW

Saw blade

Left adjustment screw

Guide rail

Tighten left adjustment screw and loosen the right screw to move the end of the fence to the left. Reverse this process to move the rear of the fence to the right.

FENCE HEAD
HEAD BLOCK
F

Spacer block
Assembled fence

⅛" holes (Mating holes are ⅛" holes 1¾" deep.)

FINGER CLAMP
E

1½" drywall screw

⁷⁄₆₄" holes

THREADED INSERT DETAIL
F
G
1¾"

2½" drywall screws
ALIGNING BLOCK

⁷⁄₆₄" pilot hole ¾" deep

⁷⁄₁₆" hole 2" deep

⅜" dowel 1¼" long

¼ × 1½" hex-head machine screw

¼" threaded insert

¼" nut

B

With the head/aligning block assembly square with the fence, glue and screw the parts together.

8. Position the fence assembly on the guide rail and check that the locking mechanism secures the fence to the guide rail. If it doesn't, you may need to take the head assembly apart and shorten or lengthen the connecting block accordingly. Now glue and screw

the assembly back together, checking for square.

9. Cut a ½ × ¾ × 2¼" stopblock to size, and glue and clamp it to the guide rail where shown on the Guide Rail Drawing, page 28. The block keeps the fence from sliding off the end of the rail.

Finish and adjust the fence

1. Mask the angle iron, and apply polyurethane to the fence assembly and guide rail. After the finish has dried, remove the tape.

2. Move the existing rear rail so the left end of the rail aligns with the saw blade where shown on the Guide Rail Drawing.

3. Position the fence assembly on the saw table and guide rail. Cut a ½ × 1 × 2¼" spacer. Glue the spacer to the bottom of the fence so the spacer rides on the rear rail. See the Fence Head Drawing, *above,* for reference.

4. Elevate your tablesaw blade as high as it will go. Slide the fence next to the blade. Using the

Fence Adjustment Drawing, *above, far left,* for reference, adjust the hex-head screws to align the fence parallel with the blade. Push the lever down, check the fence alignment to the blade, pull the lever up, adjust the screws, and recheck the alignment. Snug the ¼" nut on each screw against the ¼" threaded insert as shown in the Threaded Insert Detail, *above.*

5. Refer to the Locking Mechanism Drawing, *top left,* to secure the fence to the guide rail. When cutting plywood and other large pieces, position the fence, lock it in place, and clamp the end opposite the lock mechanism to the existing rear rail. This prevents the fence from flexing out of square.

DOUBLE-DUTY TABLESAW EXTENSIONS

M ost projects center on the tablesaw. To make your tablesaw an even more versatile workshop hub, we designed two extensions to increase the work surface. Half of one extension drops down out of the way when not in use. We also built in a router table as part of the other extension.

Note: These extensions fit a Sears 10″ tablesaw; dimensions may vary for your particular saw. Also, some models such as the Delta (formerly Rockwell) 9″ contractor's saw may require an extra hole or recess on the bottom of the back extension for the motor when tilted in the full 45° position. This design works best for a permanently mounted router. If you'll need the router for other tasks, mount it to a router plate as shown on pages 41–47.

Start with the extensions

1. First remove any factory-made metal extensions from your tablesaw. Leave the rip-fence rails in place. On a half sheet of ¾″ AA or AB plywood, measure and mark the layout of the main extension (A) and the side extension (B), shown and dimensioned in the Cutting Diagram, *opposite*. (Also mark a cutout for the blade guard on the main extension.) Cut the extensions (A, B) to size and shape (you will cut the main extension [A] in two later).

2. Trace the outline of both extensions onto the balance sheet. (The balance sheet stabilizes the extensions and reduces the chances of warpage.

If balance sheet is difficult to locate in your area, use laminate on the bottom side of the extensions.) Then score and snap the balance sheet ½″ oversize. Using contact cement, apply balance sheet to the bottom of both extensions. With a router and a flush-trim bit, trim the balance sheet flush with all edges.

3. From solid birch stock, rip and crosscut the banding strips (C–K) to size plus 1″ in length. Glue and nail strips C, D, and E to the sides of the main extension, and both F's to the sides of the side extension, where shown on the Cutaway View Drawing, *opposite*. After the glue dries, scrape off excess glue, then plane or scrape the surfaces flush, being careful not to round-over the edges. Then use a backsaw to trim the ends of the banding

strips flush with the ends of the plywood. Apply the remaining banding strips (G–K) in the same manner. Be sure to avoid nailing into strips I and J where you will rip extension A later.

4. Use a compass to mark ¾″ radii on all outside corners of the extensions, where shown in the Top View Drawing, page 34. Cut the corners to shape and sand them smooth.

5. Make a couple of marks 13¾″ from the 48″ side of the main extension to locate the hinge line. Using the marks as a guide, rip the extension in two. You will reattach the long, straight outside piece with a continuous hinge later.

6. Lay the extensions on the laminate and trace their outlines. Cut the laminate ½″ oversize and apply it to the top of the three

CUTAWAY VIEW

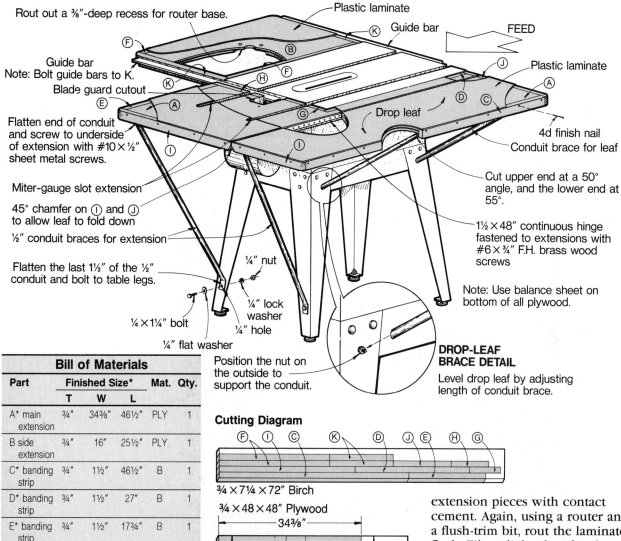

Rout out a ⅜"-deep recess for router base.

Plastic laminate

Guide bar

FEED

Guide bar
Note: Bolt guide bars to K.

Blade guard cutout

Plastic laminate

Drop leaf

Flatten end of conduit and screw to underside of extension with #10 × ½" sheet metal screws.

4d finish nail
Conduit brace for leaf

Miter-gauge slot extension

45° chamfer on ⓘ and ⓙ to allow leaf to fold down

½" conduit braces for extension

Flatten the last 1½" of the ½" conduit and bolt to table legs.

Cut upper end at a 50° angle, and the lower end at 55°.

1½ × 48" continuous hinge fastened to extensions with #6 × ¾" F.H. brass wood screws

Note: Use balance sheet on bottom of all plywood.

¼" nut

¼ × 1¼" bolt

¼" lock washer

¼" hole

¼" flat washer

Position the nut on the outside to support the conduit.

DROP-LEAF BRACE DETAIL

Level drop leaf by adjusting length of conduit brace.

Bill of Materials

Part	Finished Size*			Mat.	Qty.
	T	W	L		
A* main extension	¾"	34⅜"	46½"	PLY	1
B side extension	¾"	16"	25½"	PLY	1
C* banding strip	¾"	1½"	46½"	B	1
D* banding strip	¾"	1½"	27"	B	1
E* banding strip	¾"	1½"	17¾"	B	1
F* banding strip	¾"	1½"	25½"	B	2
G* banding strip	¾"	1½"	7⅞"	B	1
H* banding strip	¾"	1½"	8¾"	B	1
I* banding strip	¾"	1½"	36"	B	1
J* banding strip	¾"	1½"	16"	B	1
K* banding strip	¾"	1½"	17½"	B	2

*Parts marked with an * are cut larger initially, then trimmed to finished size. Please read the instructions before cutting.

Material Key: PLY—plywood, B—birch.
Supplies: 4×4' balance sheet, 4×4' plastic laminate, contact cement, 4d finish nails, 2—10' lengths of ½" conduit, 1½×48" continuous hinge with #6×¾" flathead brass wood screws, 4—broomstick holders, #10×½" sheet-metal screws, 2—¼×1¼" bolts with flat washers/lock washers/nuts, oil or polyurethane finish, 4—lag screws and washers.

Cutting Diagram

¾ × 7¼ × 72" Birch

¾ × 48 × 48" Plywood

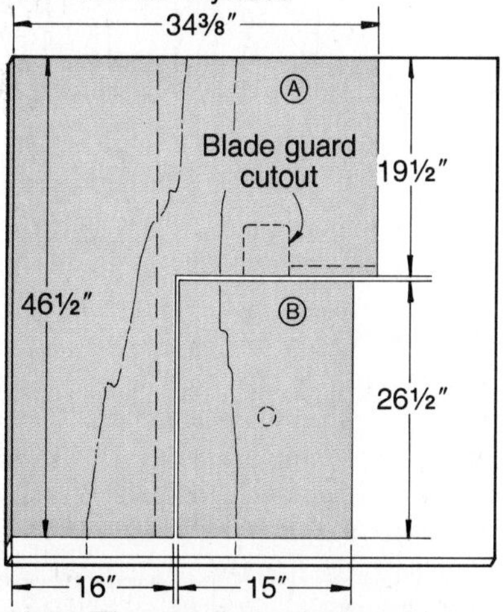

34⅜"

Blade guard cutout

19½"

46½"

26½"

16"   15"

Note: The plastic laminate and balance sheet are cut slightly larger than the plywood, then trimmed to final size with a router.

extension pieces with contact cement. Again, using a router and a flush-trim bit, rout the laminate flush. File a slight chamfer along the top edge of the three laminate pieces to dull the sharp edge.

7. Chamfer the mating ends of banding strips I and J where shown in the Cutaway View Drawing so you will be able to fold down the drop-leaf portion of the main extension. (We used a combination square to mark the 45° angles on the banding strips. Then we cut the chamfers with a handsaw and sanded the edges smooth.)

Prepare the extensions for mounting

1. Apply masking tape to the sides and back of the top surface of the saw table, where shown on the Marking the *continued*

DOUBLE-DUTY TABLESAW EXTENSIONS
continued

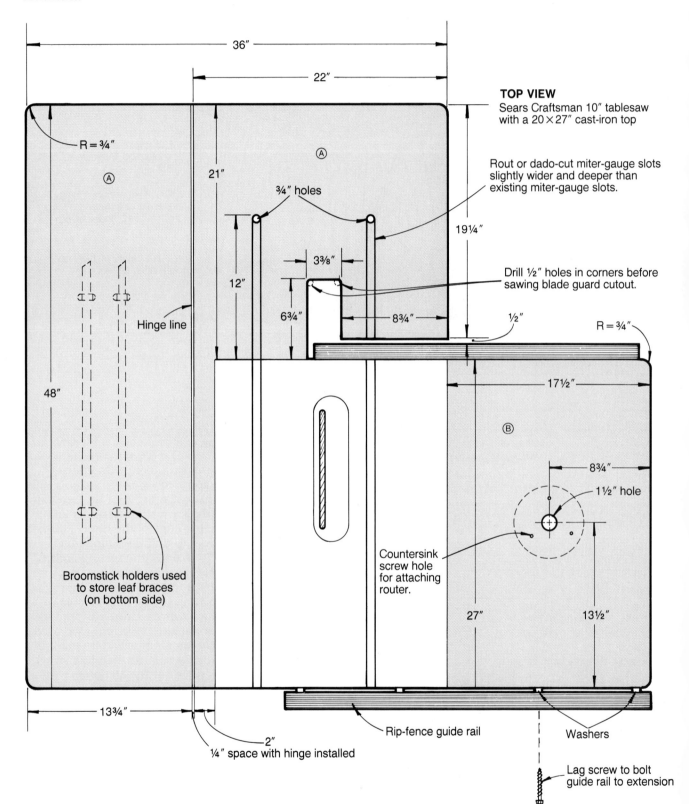

TOP VIEW
Sears Craftsman 10″ tablesaw with a 20 × 27″ cast-iron top

36″

22″

R = ¾″

Ⓐ

Ⓐ

21″

¾″ holes

Rout or dado-cut miter-gauge slots slightly wider and deeper than existing miter-gauge slots.

19¼″

3⅜″

12″

Drill ½″ holes in corners before sawing blade guard cutout.

6¾″

8¾″

½″

R = ¾″

Hinge line

17½″

Ⓑ

48″

8¾″

1½″ hole

Broomstick holders used to store leaf braces (on bottom side)

Countersink screw hole for attaching router.

27″

13½″

13¾″

2″

¼″ space with hinge installed

Rip-fence guide rail

Washers

Lag screw to bolt guide rail to extension

Mounting Holes Drawing, Step 1, *below.* (We used masking tape because it makes a better marking surface.) Then use a square to transfer the location of the center of each hole to the masking tape.

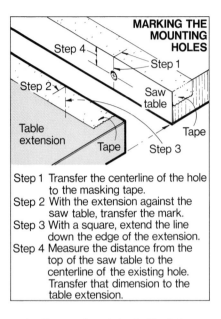

MARKING THE MOUNTING HOLES

Step 4
Step 1
Step 2
Saw table
Table extension
Tape
Tape
Step 3

Step 1 Transfer the centerline of the hole to the masking tape.
Step 2 With the extension against the saw table, transfer the mark.
Step 3 With a square, extend the line down the edge of the extension.
Step 4 Measure the distance from the top of the saw table to the centerline of the existing hole. Transfer that dimension to the table extension.

2. Clamp the right half of the main extension to your saw table, using a helper to hold it in position. Apply tape to the adjoining surface of the extension and continue the lines onto the extension (Step 2 in drawing). Follow steps 3 and 4 to finish marking the mounting-hole locations.

3. Using the Top View Drawing, *opposite,* as a guide, mark the position of the miter-gauge slot extensions and the blade-guard cutout. The slots should extend onto the main extension where shown.

4. Using the method just described for the main extension, clamp the side extension to the saw and mark the mounting holes. Then unclamp both extensions from the saw.

5. Drill $5/16''$ holes through the edge of the extensions where marked. Using a flat-bottomed bit, drill 1" holes $\frac{1}{2}''$ deep in the bottom of each extension, centered on the $5/16''$ holes just drilled (see the How to Attach the Extension Drawing, *top right*).

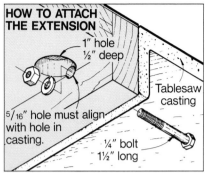

HOW TO ATTACH THE EXTENSION

1" hole $\frac{1}{2}''$ deep

$5/16''$ hole must align with hole in casting.

Tablesaw casting

$\frac{1}{4}''$ bolt $1\frac{1}{2}''$ long

6. Cut the slots where marked in the main extension, making them slightly wider and deeper than the existing miter-gauge slots in your saw table. (To avoid chipping the laminate, use a carbide-tipped straight bit in your router. Clamp a straight board to the extension as a fence when routing the slots.) Drill $\frac{3}{4}''$ holes through the extension at the end of each slot, backing the holes with scrap to prevent chip-out. (The holes help eliminate sawdust pileup in the slots.)

7. Screw the continuous hinge to both sections of the main extension, making sure the ends and top surfaces of each are flush.

8. Place the side extension, laminate side down, on a work surface. Locate and mark the centerpoint of the router-base recess where shown in the Top View Drawing. Drill a $\frac{1}{8}''$ hole at this point. Rout a $\frac{3}{8}''$-deep recess to house the router base. Flip the extension right side up and drill a $1\frac{1}{2}''$ hole with a holesaw, using the $\frac{1}{8}''$ hole as a centerpoint.

9. To mount the router to the bottom of the extension, first remove the plastic base from the router. Place the router into the router recess. Then mark and drill the router-mounting holes (the ones used to attach the plastic subbase). Countersink the mounting holes from the top side to recess the router-mounting screws slightly below the top of the surface. (The location and size of the screws may vary depending on your router.)

10. Sand the edges of both extensions smooth, and apply finish to the exposed banding.

Mount the extensions

1. Bolt the side extension to the saw table, checking that the surfaces are flush. (We clamped a straight piece of scrap across the saw table and over the extension to true the two surfaces. We also used slightly smaller nuts and bolts than those used with the original extensions. This allows for minor adjustments when trueing the surfaces.)

2. Bolt the extension to the rip-fence guide rails. (We drilled pilot holes and used lag screws to bolt the rails to the extensions. We also placed washers between the front guide rail and side extension.)

3. Bolt the main extension to the saw table (don't put a lot of weight on it until you brace). Measure the length of conduit needed for the two back braces. Cut the conduit to length.

4. Using a vise or mallet, flatten the top and the bottom $1\frac{1}{2}''$ of each of the back braces. Drill a $3/16''$ hole through the top flattened end and a $\frac{1}{4}''$ hole through the bottom. Making sure the extension rests level with the saw table, position one of the braces under the back extension. Bend the flattened ends to fit against one of the legs and the inside edge of I. Drill a hole through the leg, and bolt the brace to the leg where shown in the Cutaway View Drawing, page 33. Screw the top of the brace to the underside of the extension. Repeat for the other back brace.

5. The drop-leaf braces sit flush against the inside edge of banding piece C. Turn one of the nuts and bolts around on the leg assembly where shown in the Drop-Leaf Brace Detail, page 33. The bottom of each brace sits on the exposed nut on the leg. Cut the top and bottom of the side braces at an angle for a flush fit against the pieces they will mate with. Position the braces on the nuts and under the hinged extension.

6. Attach broomstick holders to the bottom of the leaf to store the braces when the leaf is folded.

BLADE-HEIGHT GAUGE

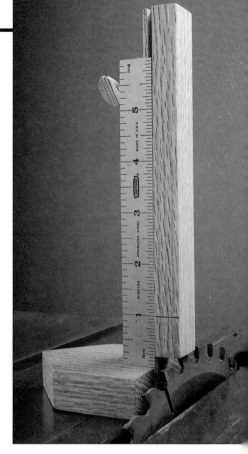

Not long ago, one of our woodworking friends claimed that "a shop aid that really works is worth its weight in ebony." We couldn't agree more. That's why we're so anxious to share this blade-height gauge with you. With it, you can easily set your tablesaw blade to exactly the right height.

Note: When cutting the parts, we cut everything extra long for machining safety. By cutting to the lengths stated, you'll have enough material for an extra gauge—perhaps for a woodworking friend.

Construct the support and sliding bar

1. Cut a piece of ¾"-thick oak to ⅝" wide by 14" long for the support (A). Cut a ½" groove ⅛" deep centered along one edge where shown on the Step 1 Drawing, *below*.

2. Rip a ⅛"-thick strip from the edge of a piece of ¾" oak stock, and crosscut it to 14" for part B.

3. Rub paraffin wax on the inside edges of the ⅛" groove you cut in part A (this will help keep the glue from sticking to them). With the edges of parts A and B flush, apply glue sparingly,

and clamp them together (see the Step 2 Drawing, *below*). Immediately after clamping, remove any glue from the groove with a thin piece of wood.

4. Using a ¼" dado blade, cut a ¼" kerf centered from side to side the length of the support where shown on the Step 3 Drawing, *bottom right*.

5. Cut a 6¾" piece from the lamination (don't forget, you'll have enough material for two supports).

6. Drill a ⅜" hole through the support (A) where shown on the Exploded View Drawing, *opposite*. Don't drill through the two strips (B).

7. Cut a piece of ¾"-thick oak to ¹³⁄₁₆ × 14". Follow drawings for steps 4, 5, and 6, *opposite,* to form the sliding bar (C). (Note that the kerfs in the sliding bar are offset to align one edge of the bar flush with the surface of the metal rule.) Check the sliding bar's fit in the support, and sand the mating edges if necessary. Cut the sliding bar to length.

Laminate and cut the base

1. Cut a piece of ¾"-thick oak stock to ¾" wide by 19" long for the base (D). Cut three 3" strips from this piece.

2. Position three strips around the support where shown on the

drawing *below*. Mark a reference line across the top of the two outer strips. Spread a thin film of glue on the mating edges, realign the pieces (without the support

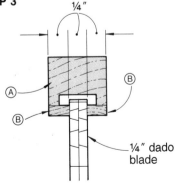

Reference line / Back edges flush

STEP 1

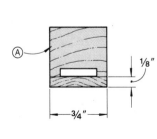

STEP 2

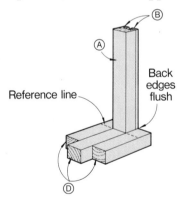

STEP 3

Bill of Materials

Part	Finished Size* T	W	L	Mat.	Qty.
A* support	¾″	⅝″	6¾″	O	1
B* strip	⅛″	¼″	6¾″	O	2
C* sliding bar	¾″	13/16″	6¾″	O	1
D* base	¾″	2¼″	3″	LO	1

*Parts marked with an * are cut larger initially, then trimmed to finished size. Please read the instructions before cutting.

Material Key: O—oak, LO—laminated oak.
Supplies: 2—¾″-diameter round magnets, epoxy, ¼″ thumbscrew ½″ long, 6″ metal rule (Sears catalog no. 9GT40136), paraffin wax, ¼″ threaded insert, 3/16″ dowel stock, finish.

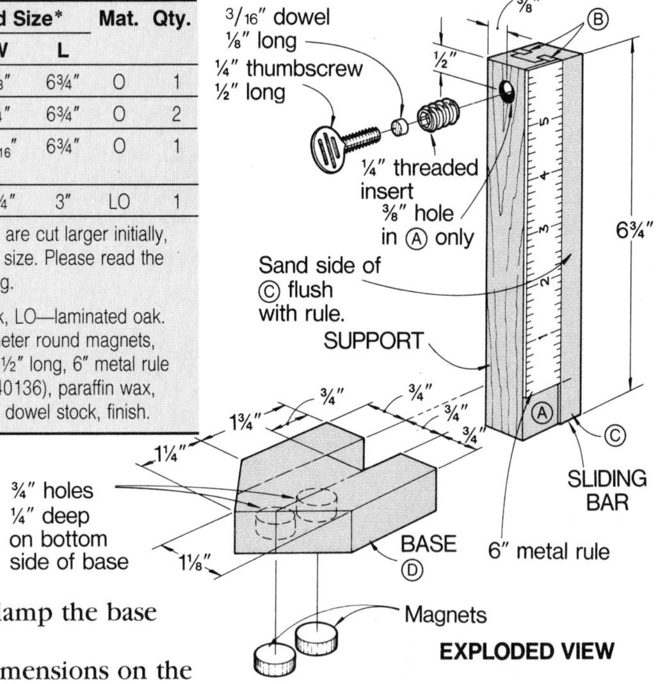

3/16″ dowel
⅛″ long
¼″ thumbscrew
½″ long
¼″ threaded insert
⅜″ hole
in Ⓐ only
Sand side of
Ⓒ flush
with rule.
SUPPORT
⅜″
½″
Ⓑ
6¾″
1¾″
¾″
¾″
¾″
¾″
1¼″
Ⓐ
Ⓒ
SLIDING BAR
¾″ holes
¼″ deep
on bottom
side of base
1⅛″
BASE
Ⓓ
6″ metal rule
Magnets

EXPLODED VIEW

this time), and clamp the base pieces together.

3. Using the dimensions on the Exploded View Drawing, mark the shape of the base on the lamination, and bandsaw it.

4. Using a flat-bottomed bit (we used a Forstner bit), bore a pair of ¾″ holes ¼″ deep on the bottom of the base for the magnets.

5. Epoxy the magnets in place in the ¾″-diameter holes in the base (see the Buying Guide for our source). When the epoxy is dry, sand the bottom of the base flush with the magnets.

Assemble the gauge

1. Glue the support into the notch of the base, checking for square.

2. Sand the back of the rule for better adhesion. Epoxy the metal rule to the support where shown on the Exploded View Drawing (the bottom edge of the rule should be flush with the top of the base).

3. Finish-sand all the pieces.

4. Screw a ¼″ threaded insert into the ⅜″ hole in the support. Don't screw the threaded insert into the grooved area. Cut a ⅛″ length from a 3/16″-diameter dowel (to prevent the thumbscrew from marring the sliding bar).

5. Position the bottom edge of the support flush with that of the sliding bar. Use a square and a hobby knife to scribe a line across the sliding bar even with the bottom edge of the metal rule as shown in the photo, *top right*. Darken the scribed line with

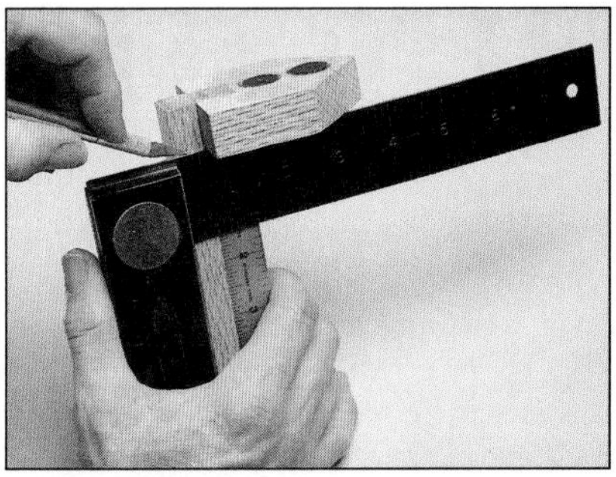

Scribe a line across the sliding bar even with the bottom of the rule.

pencil lead. Mask off the rule, magnets, and threaded insert, and apply a clear finish.

6. To allow the bar to slide freely in the support, wax the mating edges, and fit the sliding bar into the groove in the support. Place the 3/16″ dowel in the hole in the threaded insert. Thread the thumbscrew into the threaded insert.

Putting the gauge to use

Position the height gauge on the tablesaw with the sliding bar above the highest point of the blade (directly above the arbor). Raise the blade, which raises the sliding bar, until the scribed line matches the desired height.

Buying Guide

- **Height-gauge hardware kit.** 6″ metal rule, 2 disk magnets, ¼″ thumbscrew, ¼″ threaded insert. Catalog no. 105HG. For current price, contact Puckett Electric Tools, 841 Eleventh St., Des Moines, IA 50309, or call 800-544-4189 or 515/244-4189.

STEP 4

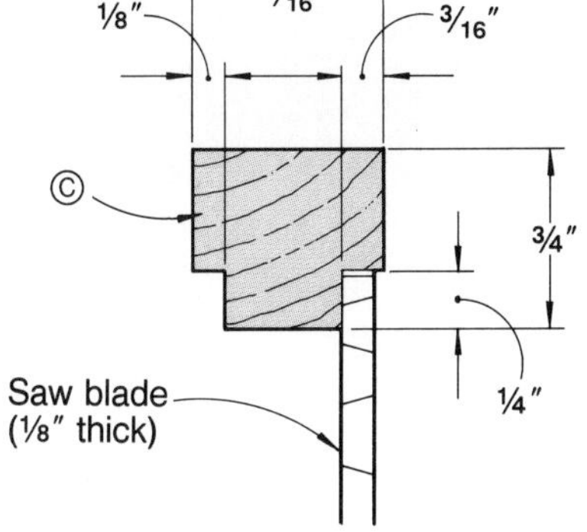

13/16″
⅛″
3/16″
Ⓒ
¾″
¼″
Saw blade
(⅛″ thick)

STEP 5

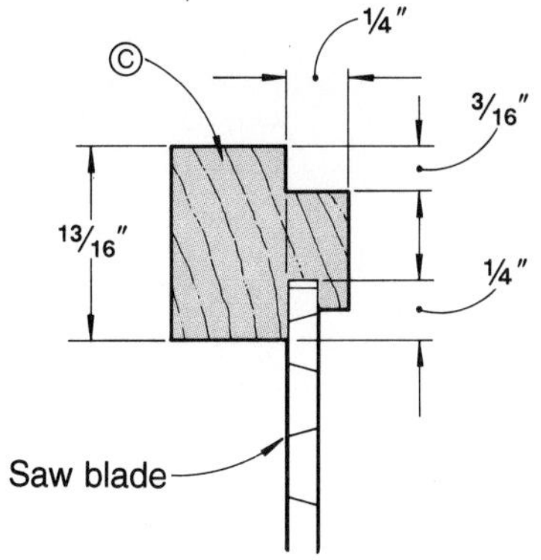

¼″
Ⓒ
3/16″
13/16″
¼″
Saw blade

STEP 6

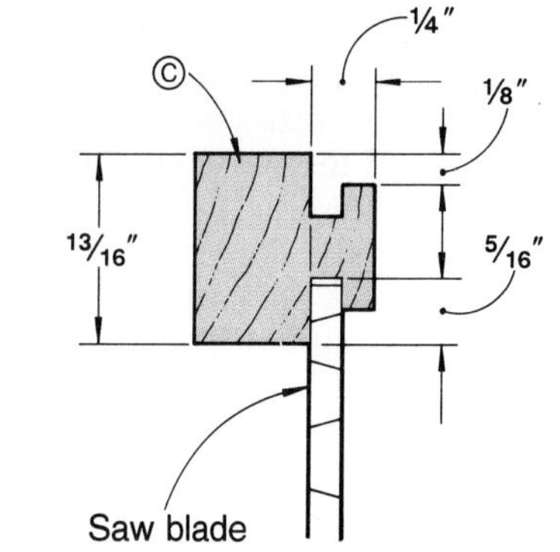

¼″
Ⓒ
⅛″
13/16″
5/16″
Saw blade

BENCHTOP ROUTER TABLE

The perfect companion to your shop's most versatile tool, this go-anywhere, bench-top router table helps make even tough routing jobs easy.

To enable you to use your router away from the router table, we've replaced the router subbase with a large acrylic router plate (see the Buying Guide on page 40 for our source). To keep your shop clean and your lungs clear, connect your vacuum hose to the vacuum-hose adapter on both the fence and guard.

The fence works well when routing straight pieces such as decorative molding. The guard, designed for use with router bits that have pilot bearings, performs best when routing the edge of an irregularly shaped object.

Note that this is the first of four router-accessory projects. If your router is a heavy-duty model, consider building the cabinet-size base featured on pages 41–47. We also show how to construct a pin-routing attachment (pages 48–50) and a box-joint jig (pages 51–53).

Construct the base

1. Rip and crosscut the feet (A), leg parts (B, C), and support frame pieces (D, E) to the sizes listed in the Bill of Materials.

2. Glue and clamp together the legs (B, C) in a T-shape, with part C centered on and flush with the ends of part B.

3. Cut half-lap joints at each end of the support frame pieces (D, E). We did the work with a radial-arm saw fitted with a dado blade. We set the depth at one-half the thickness of the maple stock, clamped a length stop 3″ from the blade, made test-cuts with scrap, then made the cuts. It takes several passes with the dado blade to form each half lap.

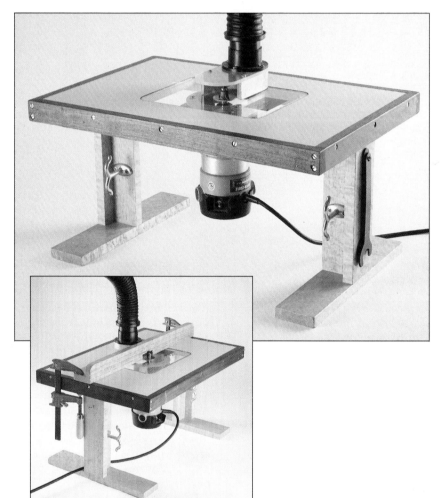

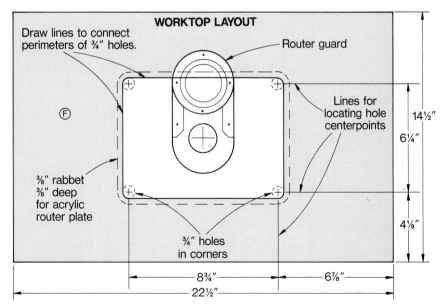

WORKTOP LAYOUT

Draw lines to connect perimeters of ¾″ holes.

Router guard

Lines for locating hole centerpoints

⅜″ rabbet ⅜″ deep for acrylic router plate

¾″ holes in corners

14½″

6¼″

4⅛″

8¾″

6⅞″

22½″

Bill of Materials

Part	Finished Size T	W	L	Mat.	Qty.
Base					
A foot	¾"	3"	14½"	M	2
B leg	¾"	3"	9¾"	M	2
C leg	¾"	2¼"	9¾"	M	2
D frame	¾"	3"	22⅜"	M	2
E frame	¾"	3"	14⅜"	M	2
Top					
F tabletop	¾"	14½"	22½"	PLY	1
G banding	¾"	1½"	24"	W	2
H banding	¾"	1½"	14½"	W	2
Fence and Guard					
I upright	¾"	2"	24"	M	1
J base	¾"	3¾"	24"	M	1
K filler block	¾"	3½"	3¾"	M	1
L chase	1¼"	3½"	5"	LM	1

Material Key: M—maple, PLY—plywood or particleboard, W—walnut, LM—laminated maple.

Supplies: #8×¾" roundhead brass wood screws, #8×1¼" flathead wood screws, #10×2" flathead wood screws, 8-32×2¼" roundhead brass machine screws, #8×1" roundhead brass wood screw, 8-32×½" roundhead brass machine screw, #8×1¼" roundhead brass wood screws, 2—brass coat hooks and mounting screws, ¼×3½×7" clear acrylic for guard, 2—15×23" pieces of plastic laminate, contact cement, finish.

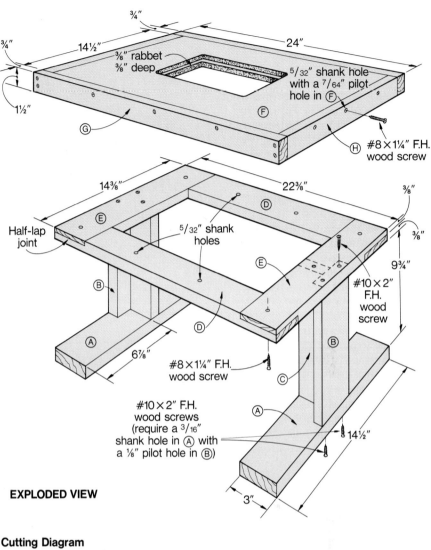

EXPLODED VIEW

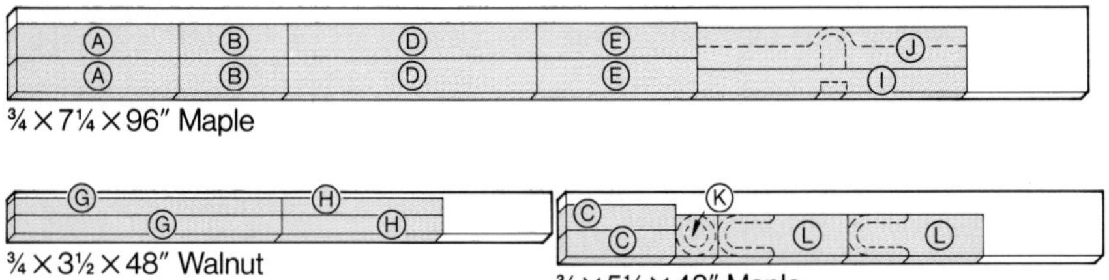

4. Glue and clamp together the support frame pieces; check them for square.

5. Clamp the legs between the feet and support frame (see the Exploded View Drawing *above right* for the correct location). Drill and countersink ⅛" pilot holes through parts A and E and 1¼" into the legs. Enlarge the top ½" of the pilot hole by drilling with a ³⁄₁₆" bit to house the screw shank. Remove the clamps, glue the mating surfaces, and install #10×2" wood screws.

Build the top

Note: We used a sink cutout for our tabletop. Often, you can buy these inexpensively at home-centers and lumberyards. If you can't find one, follow step 1 below to build your own top.

Cutting Diagram

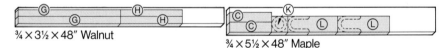

¾ × 7¼ × 96" Maple

¾ × 3½ × 48" Walnut

¾ × 5½ × 48" Maple

1. Cut the tabletop (F) to size. Cut two pieces of plastic laminate to 15×23". Using contact cement, adhere one of the plastic-laminate pieces to the top of the tabletop. With a flush-trimming bit, rout the edges of the laminate flush with the edges of the top. Repeat with the bottom piece.

2. To form the opening in the worktop (F) for the router plate, mark the centerpoints for the four ¾" holes where shown on the drawing *opposite*. Bore the holes.

Mark lines to connect the perimeters of the holes. Using a jigsaw, cut along the inside edge of the marked lines to cut the opening. Sand the opening smooth. (See the Buying Guide on page 40 for our source of a precut router plate, or have a piece of ⅜" acrylic cut to size.)

3. Rout a ⅜" rabbet ⅜" deep along the top edge of the opening. The top of the router plate needs to sit flush with the top of the tabletop. *continued*

BENCHTOP ROUTER TABLE
continued

4. Rip and crosscut the walnut banding pieces (G, H) to size. Screw them to the tabletop using #8×1¼″ flathead wood screws. Attach the tabletop to the maple base.

Build the fence and guard, and add the finish

1. Use the drawings at *right* to build the fence and guard. The fence and guard were designed to accommodate a 2¼″ vacuum-hose adapter (see the Buying Guide for our source). Dimensions may have to be adjusted to fit your vacuum.

2. Position the guard on the top, and use the ³⁄₁₆″ holes in the guard as a guide to locate the holes in the plate.

3. Sand all the wood pieces, and apply the finish. Screw the coat hooks to the legs (the hooks allow you to wrap up the router cord when not in use).

Buying Guide
• **Two vacuum-hose adapters.** Part no. 516262, from Shopsmith, 3931 Image Drive, Dayton, OH 45414. Call 800-543-7586 or 513/898-6070 for current price.

• **Router plate.** ⅜×7¾×10¼″ clear acrylic insert, radiused corners, chamfered edges, router-mounting instructions included. Catalog no. 102. If your router uses metric screws, specify router brand and model for a set of extra-long screws for mounting the router to the plate. For current prices for the router plate, extra-long screws, and ¼×3½×7″ acrylic guard plate, contact Woodhaven, 5323 W. Kimberly Rd., Davenport, IA 52806. Or call 800-344-6657 or 319/391-2386.

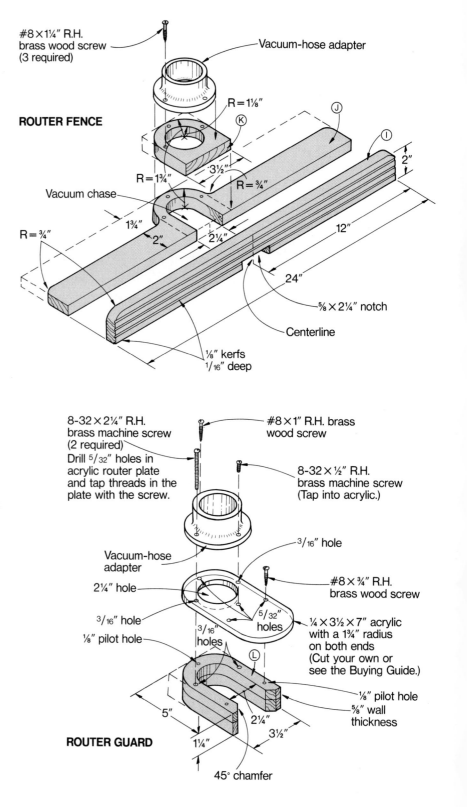

ROUTER FENCE

#8×1¼″ R.H. brass wood screw (3 required)

Vacuum-hose adapter

R=1⅛″

R=1¾″

R=¾″

Vacuum chase

R=¾″

1¾″

2″

2¼″

3½″

12″

24″

⅝×2¼″ notch

Centerline

⅛″ kerfs 1/16″ deep

ROUTER GUARD

8-32×2¼″ R.H. brass machine screw (2 required)
Drill 5/32″ holes in acrylic router plate and tap threads in the plate with the screw.

#8×1″ R.H. brass wood screw

8-32×½″ R.H. brass machine screw (Tap into acrylic.)

3/16″ hole

Vacuum-hose adapter

2¼″ hole

3/16″ hole

⅛″ pilot hole

3/16″ holes

5/32″ holes

#8×¾″ R.H. brass wood screw

¼×3½×7″ acrylic with a 1¾″ radius on both ends (Cut your own or see the Buying Guide.)

⅛″ pilot hole
⅝″ wall thickness

5″

1¼″

2¼″

3½″

45° chamfer

HEAVY-DUTY ROUTER TABLE

If you have a heavy-duty router or are thinking about buying one, and you want to build a table for it, you'll need a more substantial table than the one detailed on pages 38–40. The hefty, professional-quality router table shown here houses a 3-hp. electronic plunge router that complements the ever-increasing variety of 1/2″-shanked router bits on the market. It boasts a 24x36″ work surface and employs two vacuum pickups for a cough-free workshop. And, after you drill mounting holes, you can fit it with our pin-routing attachment shown on pages 47 and 48–50, or with the box-joint jig featured on pages 47 and 51–53.

Features everywhere . . . just take a look!

To install and remove the router from the rabbeted opening in the router table, replace your router's subbase with a large clear acrylic *router plate* (see the Buying Guide on page 47 for our source). The replacement plate also acts as a base when using the router away from the router table. This keeps you from having to change bases every time you hold the router by hand during machining operations.

To keep your shop clean and your lungs happy, connect your vacuum hose to the *upper vacuum pipe* when using the *guard* for operations such as edge molding and rabbeting. In addition, the guard helps protect the operator from the cutter and flying chips. When you're performing such operations as dadoing, grooving, and pin routing, and you can't use the guard, switch to the *lower*

vacuum pipe to remove dust from below the table and bit. (A dust-free router also lasts longer.)

Attach and align the *split fences* on either side of the guard for plenty of support when routing long pieces. Offset the fences when removing stock from the entire edge of a project. If you don't have a jointer, mount a straight bit to the router, offset the fences slightly, and joint the edges of stock.

Although you could install almost any router in this table, we chose a Ryobi *3-hp. electronic plunge model*. The electronic *speed control* on this router works

great to lower the speed for larger bits. We like the Ryobi's *depth-control knob* for ease in raising and lowering the bit. If you already have a large router, see the Buying Guide on page 47 for our source of auxiliary depth controls.

Attach the acrylic plate to the router

Note: To mount the router to the router table you'll need a piece of ⅜″ acrylic. You can buy a piece locally, or see the Buying Guide for our source of precut plates.

continued

HEAVY-DUTY ROUTER TABLE
continued

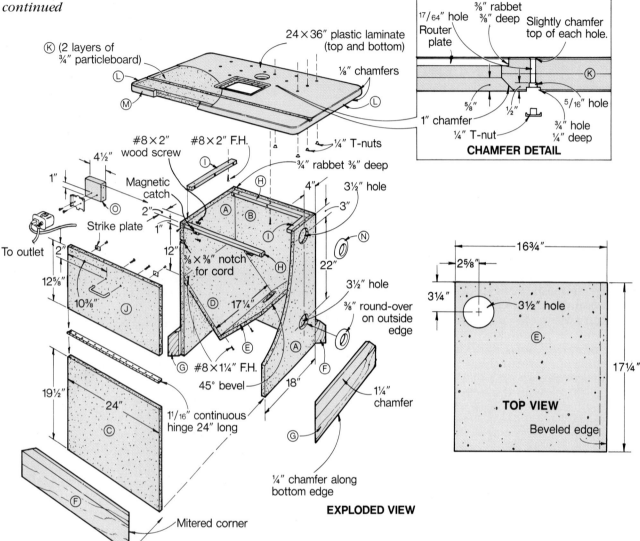

Ⓚ (2 layers of ¾" particleboard)

24×36" plastic laminate (top and bottom)

⅛" chamfers

CHAMFER DETAIL

¹⁷⁄₆₄" hole
Router plate
⅜" rabbet ⅜" deep
Slightly chamfer top of each hole.
⅝"
1" chamfer
¼" T-nut
½"
¾" hole ¼" deep
⁵⁄₁₆" hole

#8×2" wood screw
#8×2" F.H.
Magnetic catch
Strike plate
To outlet
¾" rabbet ⅜" deep
⅜"×⅜" notch for cord
4"
3½" hole
3"
3½" hole
⅜" round-over on outside edge
22"
17¼"
45° bevel
18"
1¼" chamfer
¼" chamfer along bottom edge
Mitered corner
1¹⁄₁₆" continuous hinge 24" long
#8×1¼" F.H.
24"
19½"
12⅝"
10⅜"
12"
2"
2"
1"
1"
4½"

EXPLODED VIEW

TOP VIEW
16¾"
2⅝"
3¼"
3½" hole
17¼"
Beveled edge

*Parts marked with an * are cut larger initially, then trimmed to finished size. Please read the instructions before cutting.

Material Key: PB—particleboard, P—pine, LPB—laminated particleboard, B—birch, PLY—plywood.

Supplies: #8×1" flathead wood screws, #8×1¼" flathead wood screws, #8×1¾" flathead wood screws, #8×2" flathead wood screws, #10×½" flathead wood screws, ¾" drywall screws, 1¼" drywall screws, ¼×2" roundhead machine screws, 1¹⁄₁₆" continuous hinge 24" long, panel adhesive, 90° street elbow (for 3" PVC pipe), 45° street elbow (for 3" PVC pipe), 3" PVC pipe 2' long, quick-set epoxy, 2 pieces of 25×37" plastic laminate, contact cement, four pieces of ¼" all-thread rod 4⅛" long, 4 knobs (Delta part no. 1087524, used on their miter gauge), ¼" wing nuts, ¼" flat washers, 14—¼" T-nuts, nylon pull (handle), 2 magnetic catches and plates, ¼×5×11¾" clear acrylic, 3½×3½" square corner hinge (Stanley part no. 741), ¼-20carriage bolt 2" long, ¼" steel rod 2½" long, filler, sanding sealer, paint.

Bill of Materials

Part	Finished Size*			Mat.	Qty.
	T	W	L		
Base Cabinet					
A side	¾"	18"	32½"	PB	2
B back	¾"	23¼"	32½"	PB	1
C front	¾"	19½"	24"	PB	1
D trough side (L)	¾"	17¼"	16"	PB	1
E trough side (R)	¾"	17¼"	16¾"	PB	1
F* front and back	1½"	5½"	27"	B	2
G* side	1½"	5½"	21¾"	B	2
H cleat	¾"	1¼"	22½"	P	2
I cleat (side)	¾"	1¼"	14¾"	P	2
J door	¾"	12⅝"	24"	PB	1

Bill of Materials (continued)

Part	Finished Size*			Mat.	Qty.
	T	W	L		
Worktop					
K* panel	1½"	22½"	34½"	LPB	1
L side banding	¾"	1½"	22½"	B	2
M banding	¾"	1½"	36"	B	2
Vacuum Connector and Switch Block					
N* connector	¾"	4" diam.		PB	2
O switch block	1½"	4"	4½"	B	1
Fences and Guard					
P base	¾"	5"	7"	PLY	2
Q support	¾"	2"	7"	PLY	2
R guide	¾"	2"	16½"	B	2
S side	¾"	2⅛"	8¼"	B	2
T back	¾"	2⅛"	4¼"	B	1

Cutting Diagram

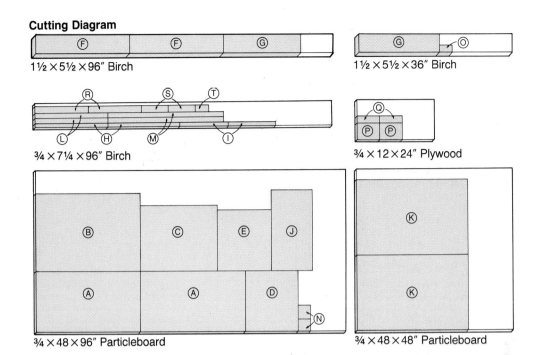

1½ × 5½ × 96″ Birch

1½ × 5½ × 36″ Birch

¾ × 7¼ × 96″ Birch

¾ × 12 × 24″ Plywood

¾ × 48 × 96″ Particleboard

¾ × 48 × 48″ Particleboard

1. Remove the subbase from your router. Center and secure the ⅜″ acrylic plate to your tool. Locate and scribe the mounting-hole centerpoints on the plate. Remove the plate from the router, and drill and countersink the holes to size.

2. Attach the router plate to your router. If you need longer screws to fasten the plate, our router plate supplier can provide them. See the Buying Guide for details.

3. Chuck a ¼″ straight bit into your router, and slowly plunge the bit through the plate. Remove the plate from the router, and use a circle cutter to cut a hole, centered over the ¼″ routed hole, large enough for your biggest bit (our hole measures 2″ in diameter).

Begin with the base cabinet

1. Cut the two side panels (A), back (B), and front (C) to the sizes listed in the Bill of Materials from ¾″-thick particleboard.

2. Cut a ¾″ rabbet ⅜″ deep along the back edge of each side panel.

3. Glue and clamp the back into the rabbet and between the side panels. Clamp the front panel to the front of the side panels, checking for square. After the glue dries, remove the clamps and sand the joints.

4. Cut the trough sides (D, E) to size, bevel-ripping the top edge of each at 45°. Using the Top View Drawing, *opposite,* for reference, mark the vacuum-hole centerpoint on the right-hand trough side (E). Mark the 3½″ hole with a compass. Cut the hole to size with a jigsaw. Referring to the dimensions on the Exploded View Drawing, *opposite,* mark the locations, and saw a pair of vacuum holes in the cabinet side (A).

5. Cut the base-surround parts (F, G) to size plus 2″ in length. (We chose birch stock; you also could use good-quality 2×6 material.) Bevel-rip a 1¼″ chamfer along the top outside edge and a ¼″ chamfer on the bottom outside edge of each piece. Miter-cut the pieces to length, and glue and clamp them to the bottom of the cabinet.

6. Glue and screw together the trough parts (D, E). Set the cabinet on its back, and slide the trough assembly into the cabinet so the top of the trough is 13″

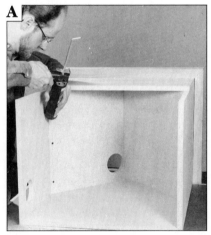

A

Screw the dust chute (D, E) in place, and caulk all joints for a tight seal.

from the top of the cabinet where shown on the Section View Drawing, page 45.

7. Drill mounting holes, and glue and screw the trough in position. For near airtight joints, caulk all the seams between the trough parts and the cabinet as shown in photo A, *above.* (We used panel adhesive to caulk the joints.)

8. Cut the cleats (H, I) to size. Drill the mounting holes, and glue and screw the cleats in place. *continued*

HEAVY-DUTY ROUTER TABLE
continued

9. Cut the door (J) to size. Cut a 1¹/₁₆″ continuous hinge to 24″ long, and fasten it to the bottom of the door and then to the top edge of the front panel (C).

10. Cut a notch for the power cord below the front cleat (H) where shown on the Exploded View Drawing, page 42.

Add the worktop

1. Cut two pieces of ¾″ particleboard to 23×35″ for the worktop panel (K). Glue and clamp together the pieces with the edges flush. Trim all four edges of the panel for a 22½×34½″ finished size.

2. From ¾″ birch stock, cut the banding pieces (L, M) to length. Glue and clamp the banding pieces to the laminated panel (K). With a compass, mark a ¾″ radius at each corner and cut to shape.

3. Cut two pieces of plastic laminate to 25×37″. Using contact cement, adhere one of the plastic-laminate pieces to the top of the worktop. With a flush-trimming bit, rout the edges of the laminate flush with the outside edge of the worktop. Repeat the process with the bottom piece. Rout a ⅛″ chamfer along the top and bottom of the worktop where shown on the Exploded View Drawing.

4. To form the opening for the router plate, mark the centerpoints for four ¾″ holes where shown on the Worktop Layout Drawing, *above right*. Bore the holes. Mark lines connecting the perimeters of the holes, and use a jigsaw to cut the opening to shape. Sand the opening smooth.

5. Rout a ⅜″ rabbet ⅜″ deep along the top inside edge of the opening. The top of the router plate should sit flush with the top of the worktop where shown on the Chamfer Detail, page 42.

6. To provide the necessary clearance for installing and removing the router from the worktop, rout a 1″ chamfer along the bottom of the opening where shown in the Chamfer Detail. (To maneuver the Ryobi router through the opening, start by turning the height-adjustment knob to lower the router as far from the acrylic plate as possible. Then angle the router slightly, and wiggle it through the worktop opening.)

7. Mark the location and cut the 3½″-diameter vacuum hole to size in the worktop.

Mount the worktop and rout the slot

1. Center and screw the worktop to the base where indicated on the Worktop Layout Drawing.

2. Mark the miter-gauge slot location on the top of the worktop where dimensioned on the Worktop Layout Drawing. As shown in photo B, *above right,* clamp a board to the top of the worktop as a straightedge. Then rout a slot to fit your miter gauge.

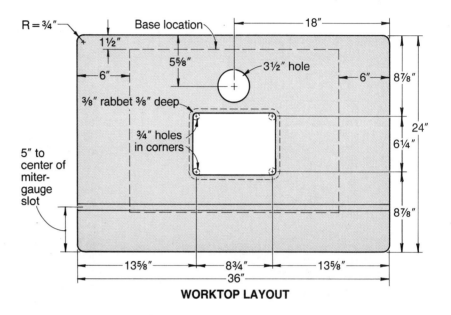

WORKTOP LAYOUT

Rout a miter-gauge groove in the worktop.

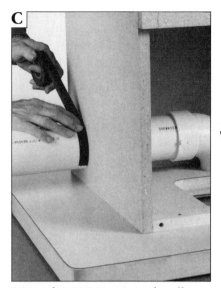

C

Insert the PVC pipe into the elbow, and mark the cutoff location with tape.

Install the dust ports

1. Position the 90° street elbow PVC pipe in the hole from the bottom of the worktop where shown in photo C, *above*. Position the cabinet on its side. Using the Section View Drawing at *right* for reference, drill two ⅛" pilot holes, and screw the 90° elbow in place.

2. Turn the cabinet upside down. Now stick a 2' length of 3" PVC pipe through the top inlet hole and into the street elbow where shown in the photo. Mark the pipe length by wrapping tape around the pipe flush with the outside surface of the cabinet side. Remove the pipe.

3. With a hacksaw, trim the 3" PVC pipe to length, cutting at the tape line. Drill a pilot hole and fasten the straight piece of pipe to the 90° street elbow. Remove the tape.

4. Repeat the procedure above to attach the lower 45° street elbow and 3" PVC pipe.

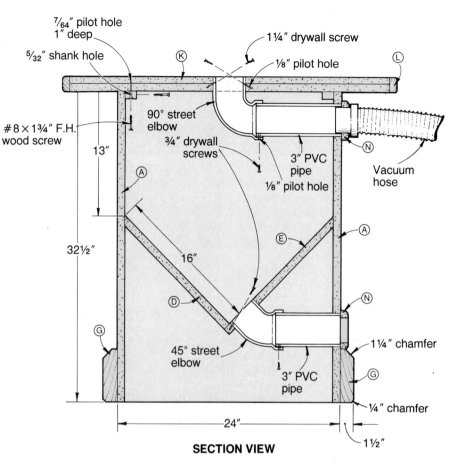

SECTION VIEW

Add the vacuum connectors and switch block

1. Cut two 4" squares from ¾" particleboard for the vacuum-hose connectors (N). Mark diagonal lines on each square to find the center.

2. Measure the outside diameter of your vacuum hose (we measured ours at 2½" with outside calipers). Using a compass, center and transfer the hole location to the connector blank. Mark a second circle ¾" on the outside of the first.

3. Drill a blade start hole and cut just inside the marked inner circle (the same diameter as your vacuum hose). Check the fit of the hose in the hole; it should fit snugly. Cut the outside circle to shape on the bandsaw and sand smooth.

4. Rout a ⅜" round-over along the top outside edge of each connector. Sand the connectors, and glue and clamp each to the cabinet, centered over the previously cut holes.

5. Cut the switch block (O) to size. With #8 × 2½" F.H. wood screws, glue and screw the block to the cabinet side (A) 6¾" from the front edge of the worktop.

HEAVY-DUTY ROUTER TABLE
continued

Build the fences

1. Cut fence base pieces (P) and supports (Q) from ¾" plywood (we used birch plywood). Cut the guides (R) to size from birch stock. Cut a ⅛ × ⅛" dust kerf along the bottom front edge of each guide.

2. Mark the slot locations on the base and support pieces, using the Fences Drawing, *top right,* for reference. Drill a ⁵⁄₁₆" hole at each end of each marked slot. With a jigsaw or scrollsaw, cut along the marked lines to form the slots.

3. Mark the centerpoints, and drill a pair of ¼" holes in each guide. Counterbore a ⅝" hole ⁵⁄₁₆" deep centered over each ¼" hole on the front face of each guide.

4. With the bottom surfaces and ends of the supports (Q) and bases (P) flush, drill the holes, and glue and screw together each assembly. Check that Q is square to P.

5. With a hacksaw, cut four pieces of ¼" all-thread rod to 3¾" long. Epoxy and thread a knob onto one end of each threaded rod (see·the Buying Guide for our source).

Construct the guard

1. Cut the guard sides (S) and back (T) to size. Cut a ¾" chamfer along the front inside edge of each side piece where dimensioned on the Router Guard Drawing, *middle right.* Cut or rout a ¾" rabbet ⅜" deep along the back inside edge of each side piece (S).

2. Glue and clamp the back piece between the side pieces. Attach the hinge to the back (T).

3. Position the router plate with attached router into the routed opening in the worktop.

4. Clamp the guard over the vacuum hole where shown on the T-Nut and Guard Location

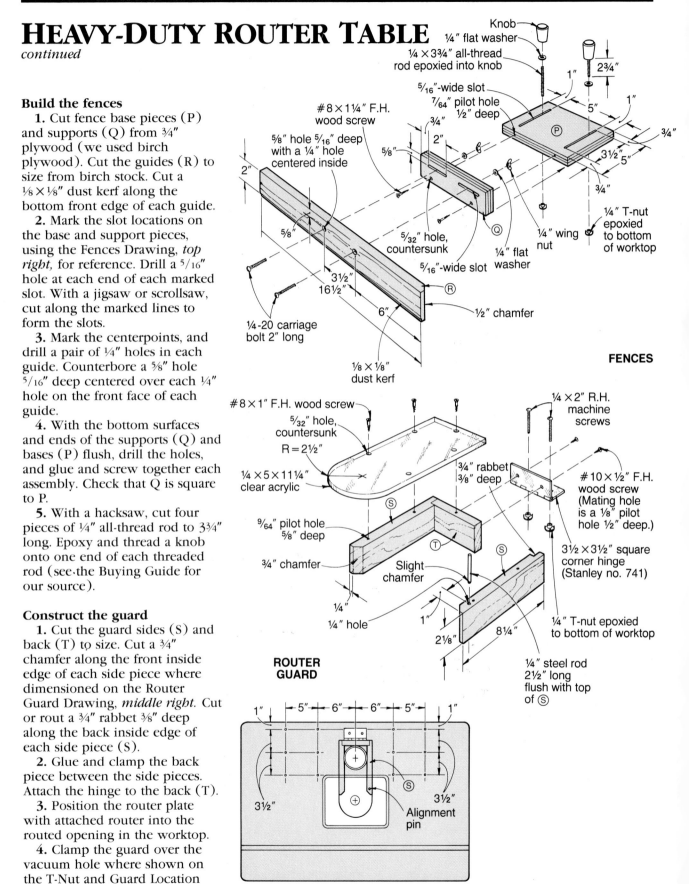

FENCES

ROUTER GUARD

T-NUT AND GUARD LOCATION

Drawing, *opposite.* Using the two outside hinge holes as guides, drill a pair of ¼" holes through the worktop.

5. With the guard clamped in place, drill a ¼" hole through the right-hand guard side (S) and through the router plate. Cut a piece of ¼" steel rod 2½" long. Grind or file a slight chamfer on the bottom end of the rod. Epoxy the rod into the hole in the guard side so ⅜" of the rod (the chamfered end) protrudes down into the hole in the router plate. Do not epoxy the rod to the plate. The rod prevents the guard from moving when stock is pushed against the guard. Remove the guard.

6. Cut the clear acrylic top to the shape shown on the Router Guard Drawing. (We used ¼" acrylic and cut it to shape with a bandsaw. See the Buying Guide for a source if you don't want to cut your own.)

7. At a speed of about 250 rpm, drill the mounting holes, and screw the acrylic to the guard assembly.

Drill the holes and add the T-nuts

1. Remove the 90° elbow from the worktop, and remove the worktop from the cabinet. On the top of the worktop, mark the T-nut-hole centerpoints where shown on the T-Nut and Guard Location Drawing. Check that the T-nut hole centerpoints align under the slots in the fence base parts (P). With a ¼" brad-point bit, drill 12 holes, backing the bottom with scrap to prevent chip-out. Switch to a ¹⁷/₆₄" bit, and enlarge the ¼" holes.

2. Countersink the holes on the top side. See the Chamfer Detail accompanying the Exploded View Drawing, page 42, for reference.

3. Turn the worktop bottom side up. Counterbore ⁵/₁₆" holes ⅜" deep centered over each ¹⁷/₆₄" hole. See the Chamfer Detail for specifics.

4. Insert a ¼" T-nut into each counterbore. Trace around the

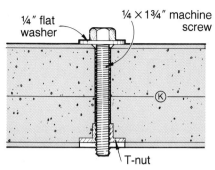

perimeter of each T-nut. With a spade bit, drill a ¾" hole ¼" deep to house the T-nut head.

5. Being careful not to get any epoxy on the interior threaded portion, epoxy each T-nut in place on the bottom side of the worktop. (Use the setup shown *above* to position each T-nut squarely until the epoxy cures.)

Apply the finish

1. Fill the voids and edges of the particleboard. (We used Durham's Rock Hard Putty.) Sand the cabinet, especially the edges, smooth.

2. Remove all the hardware, and mask the laminate top and bottom of the worktop. Next apply a coat of lacquer sanding sealer to the cabinet and guard.

3. Spray on a medium coat (no runs) of Rust-Oleum's Regal Red gloss paint, and allow it to dry until tacky. Then spray on a thicker coat. The tacky coat provides a sticky surface for the follow-up coat. Repeat the procedure twice.

4. Finally, mask mating red areas, and paint the inside with an off-white, oil-base, semigloss enamel.

Assemble the table

1. Fasten the worktop to the cabinet. Install the PVC pipe fixtures.

2. Drill the holes, and attach the door pull. Next fasten the strike plates to the back of the door and the magnetic catches to the front cleat (H). Attach the switch.

Buying Guide

• **Router plate.** ⅜ × 7¾ × 10¼" clear acrylic insert, radiused corners, and chamfered edges. Catalog no. 102. If your router uses metric screws, specify router brand and model for a set of extra-long screws for mounting router to plate. For prices, contact Woodhaven, 5323 W. Kimberly Rd., Davenport, IA 52806. Call 800-344-6657 or 319/391-2386.

• **Height-adjustment knob.** Knobs available for the Makita 3612, Bosch 1611 and 1611VS, Hitachi TR12, and Elu 3338. Woodhaven, address above.

• **Hardware kit** (for auxiliary depth controls). 4 knobs (similar to those shown) with ¼" threaded rod glued in place, 16—¼" T-nuts, nylon pull (handle), 2 magnetic catches and plates, ¼x4½ × 11¼" acrylic for guard. Woodhaven, address above.

• **Power switch.** Catalog no. A526. For current price, contact AMT, P.O. Box 70, Royersford, PA, 19468, or call 215/948-0400.

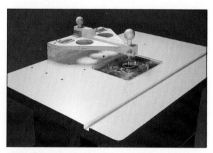

Fitted with the pin-routing attachment from pages 48–50.

Fitted with the box-joint jig featured on pages 51–53.

DELTA-WING PIN-ROUTING ATTACHMENT

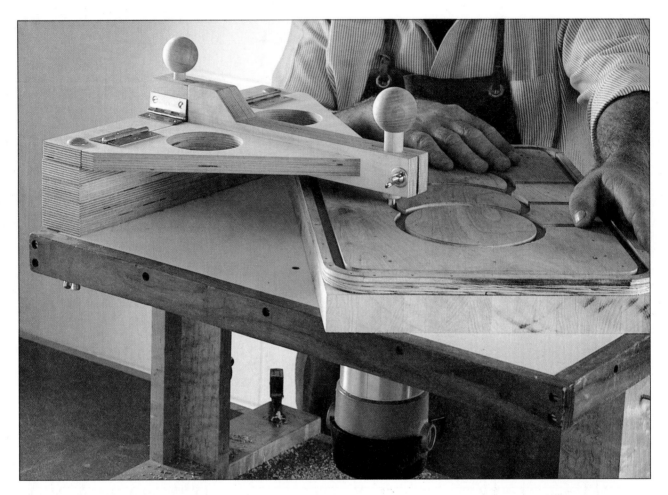

Have you ever wondered how those cutting boards or cheese trays with perfectly shaped patterns are made? Well, wonder no more. With our pin-routing attachment and a pattern or two, you can rout all the intricate projects you want.

Note: The attachment fits our router tabletop (see pages 38–40), which measures 16×24". If your table is smaller, you'll need to shorten the arm and reposition the mounting holes. It also mounts on our Heavy-Duty Router Table (see page 47).

Start with the arm and wings

1. To make the arm (A), cut two pieces of ¾" birch to 2¾×16" (we used Baltic birch plywood). Glue and clamp the pieces together face-to-face.

2. Scrape off the excess glue, and then trim or plane the edges for a 2⅝" finished width. Trim the arm to length (11¼"), and save the scrap—you'll use it later for the hold-down (D).

3. Bore a ¾" hole 1⅛" from one end, centered from side to side, in the arm where shown on the Exploded View Drawing, *opposite*. Drill a ¼" hole perpendicular to the ¾" hole ⅜" from the same end.

4. Using a bandsaw, cut the arm to the shape shown on the drawing, and sand smooth. Cut a ⅛" kerf 2¼" long centered on the joint line between the two A's, again referring to the drawing.

5. To make the wings (B), cut a piece of plywood to 7×9⁷⁄₁₆" long. Draw a diagonal across it, and cut down the center of the line to form the two wings. Cut a 3"-diameter hole in each wing where located on the drawing.

6. Cut or rout a ¾" stopped groove ⅜" deep and 8⅞" long, centered along both side edges of the arm. (We clamped a stop to the rip fence and made our grooves on the tablesaw with a

EXPLODED VIEW

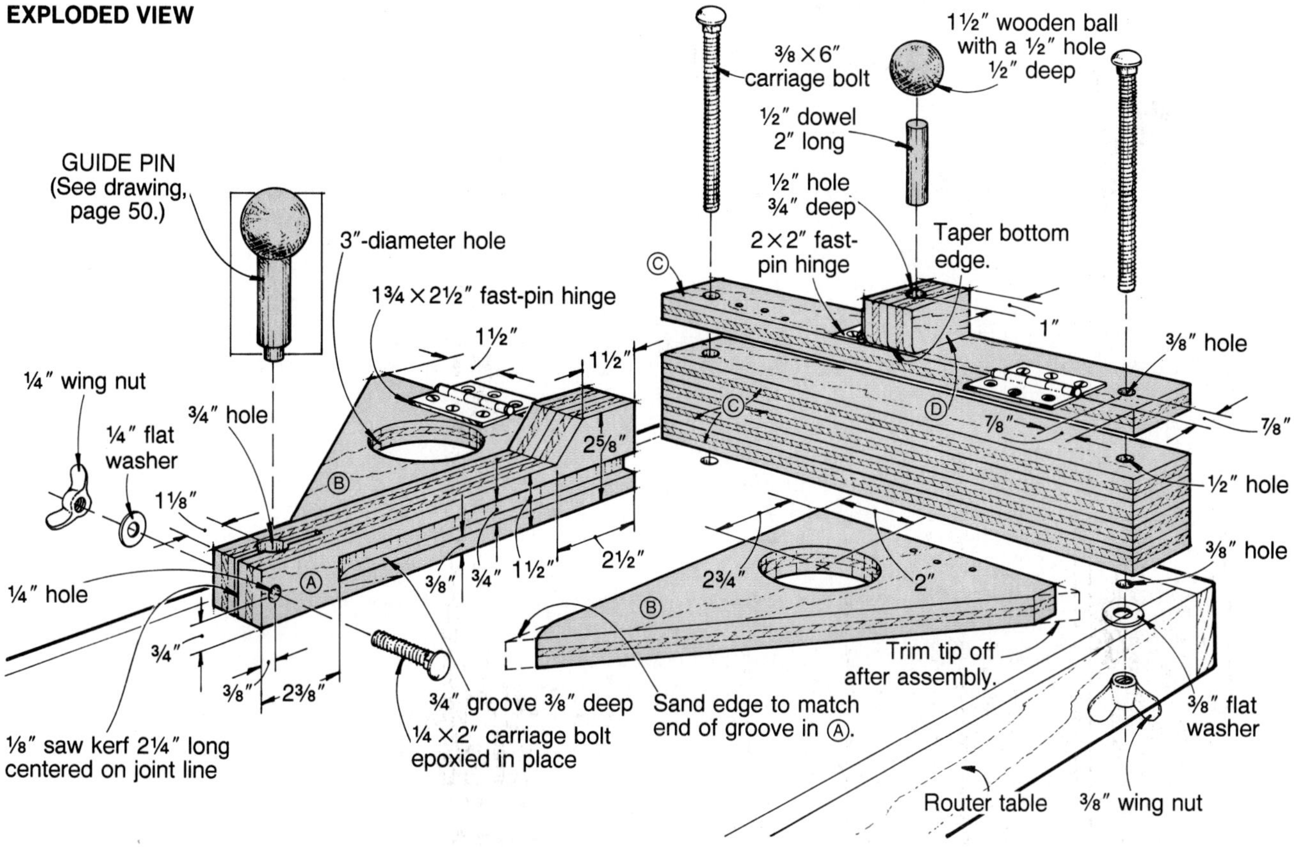
GUIDE PIN
(See drawing, page 50.)
3″-diameter hole
1¾ × 2½″ fast-pin hinge
1½″
1½″
¼″ wing nut
¾″ hole
¼″ flat washer
1⅛″
2⅝″
¼″ hole
¾″
⅜″
2⅜″
⅜″
¾″
1½″
2½″
⅛″ saw kerf 2¼″ long centered on joint line
¾″ groove ⅜″ deep
¼ × 2″ carriage bolt epoxied in place
⅜ × 6″ carriage bolt
½″ dowel 2″ long
½″ hole ¾″ deep
2 × 2″ fast-pin hinge
1½″ wooden ball with a ½″ hole ½″ deep
Taper bottom edge.
1″
⅜″ hole
⅞″
⅞″
½″ hole
⅜″ hole
2¾″
2″
Trim tip off after assembly.
Sand edge to match end of groove in Ⓐ.
⅜″ flat washer
Router table
⅜″ wing nut

dado blade. If you follow this process, sand the front edge of each wing to match the radiused end of the stopped groove.)

7. Glue and clamp the wings into the grooves in the arm (for clamping, we used a handscrew and positioned the clamping parts in the 3″ wing holes). Make sure the back edges of the wings and arm are straight and flush. Also check that the wings are level with each other.

Make the support assembly

1. Cut four spacers and the top support (C) to size. Dry-clamp the five pieces together with the edges and ends flush. Then drill a ⅜″ hole through each end of the lamination where dimensioned on the drawing. Remove the top support, reclamp the four spacers, and enlarge the holes in the spacers with a ½″ drill bit.

2. Cut the hold-down (D) to size from the scrap left over from the arm lamination. Bore a ½″ hole ¾″ deep in the hold-down where shown on the Exploded View Drawing. Sand a slight taper on the bottom front edge of the hold-down. The taper makes it easier for the hold-down to force the arm down for routing.

3. Clamp a 1½″ wooden ball (available from toy-part suppliers) in a handscrew clamp. Bore a ½″ hole ½″ deep into it. Cut a piece of ½″ dowel to 2″. Glue one end of the dowel into the hole in the ball, and the other end into the hold-down.

continued

Bill of Materials

Part	Finished Size* T	W	L	Mat.	Qty.
A* arm	1½″	2⅝″	11¼″	LB	1
B* wing	¾″	6⅝″	8⅞″	B	2
C support/ spacer	¾″	2″	14″	B	5
D* hold-down	1½″	1½″	2″	LB	1

*Parts marked with an * are cut larger initially, then trimmed to finished size. Please read the instructions before cutting.

Material Key: LB—laminated birch, B—birch.
Supplies: 2—⅜ × 6″ carriage bolts with flat washers and wing nuts, ¼ × 2″ carriage bolt with flat washer and wing nut, ¼ × 2½″ carriage bolt for the alignment pin, ⅜ × 2″ carriage bolt for guide pin, 2—1¾ × 2½″ fast-pin hinges with mounting screws, 2 × 2″ fast-pin hinge with mounting screws, 1½″ wooden ball, 2—1¾″ wooden balls, ½″ dowel, ¾″ dowel, epoxy, finish.

DELTA-WING PIN-ROUTING ATTACHMENT
continued

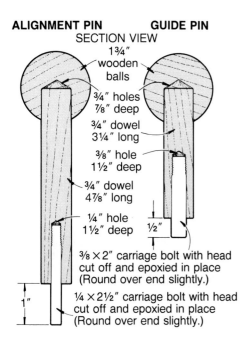

ALIGNMENT PIN   **GUIDE PIN**
SECTION VIEW

1¾"
wooden
balls

¾" holes
⅞" deep

¾" dowel
3¼" long

⅜" hole
1½" deep

¾" dowel
4⅞" long

¼" hole
1½" deep

½"

⅜ × 2" carriage bolt with head
cut off and epoxied in place
(Round over end slightly.)

¼ × 2½" carriage bolt with head
cut off and epoxied in place
(Round over end slightly.)

1"

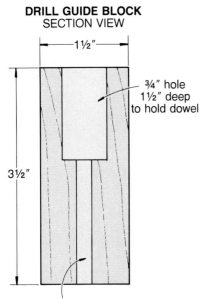

DRILL GUIDE BLOCK
SECTION VIEW

1½"

¾" hole
1½" deep
to hold dowel

3½"

¼" hole for alignment pin and a ⅜" hole
for guide pin to guide drill bit

Construct the guide and alignment pins

Note: The alignment pin *aligns the attachment with the router collet. You also can use the alignment pin as a guide pin when routing with ¼"-diameter bits. The* guide pin, *when positioned in the arm, tracks the template pattern when routing.*

1. To make the alignment pin, illustrated at *far left,* cut a piece of ¾" dowel to 4⅞" long. Using a drill guide block (see the Drill Guide Block Drawing, *bottom left,* for details on how to make one), drill a ¼" hole 1½" deep, centered in the end of the ¾" dowel. (We fit one end of the alignment pin in the ¾" hole in the guide block. Then we used the ¼" hole in the guide block to center the drill bit into the end of the alignment pin.)

2. Cut the head off a ¼ × 2½" carriage bolt. Epoxy the threaded end of the bolt into the hole in the dowel so 1" of the bolt protrudes. File a round-over on the protruding end of the bolt.

3. Clamp a 1¾" wooden ball in a handscrew, and bore a ¾" hole ⅞" deep into the ball. Glue the ball onto the end of the dowel.

4. To make the guide pin, repeat steps 1 through 3 above, using a ⅜ × 2" carriage bolt, a drill guide block with a ⅜" hole, and the Guide Pin Drawing, *above, near left.*

Assemble, finish, and mount the attachment

1. Center the arm and wing assembly against the front edge of the top support. Clamp them together, drill hinge holes, and hinge the assembly to the top support. (To ensure a snug fit between the wing assembly and top support, drill the hinge holes in the top support slightly off-center toward the back.) Trim the wing ends flush with the ends of the top support.

2. Position the hold-down on the top support, align it with the arm, and clamp it into place. Drill mounting holes, and hinge the hold-down to the top support firmly against the back edge of the arm.

3. Place the alignment pin into the ¾" hole in the arm. Epoxy a ¼ × 2" carriage bolt in the ¼" hole at the kerfed end of the arm, and attach a flat washer and wing nut to the bolt to hold it secure until the epoxy dries. Finish the pin router as desired. (We disassembled the parts, masked off the hinges, and applied polyurethane to the supports, wing assembly, and pins.)

4. Raise your table-mounted router so the collet protrudes slightly above the surface of the table. Position the pin-routing attachment (with a couple of spacers beneath it) so the alignment pin fits into the collet as shown in the illustration *below.* Clamp the pin router to the router table. Using the holes in the spacers as guides, drill two ⅜" holes through the router table. Fasten the routing attachment to the router table with a pair of carriage bolts.

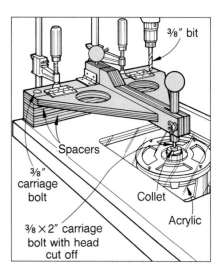

⅜" bit

Spacers

⅜"
carriage
bolt

Collet

Acrylic

⅜ × 2" carriage
bolt with head
cut off

ACCURATE BOX-JOINT JIG

You'll seldom meet a woodworker who doesn't appreciate the good looks and durability of a box joint (also called a finger joint). But most woodworkers hate all the setup fuss. Wilbur Rath, a retired dairy farmer from Shiocton, Wisconsin, took the problem to heart. Use his design with a tablesaw, as shown at *right,* or with our Heavy-Duty Router Table (see page 47).

Form the sliding block and carriage

1. Rip and crosscut the sliding block parts (A, B) and carriage parts (C) to the sizes listed in the Bill of Materials, page 52.

2. Cut or rout a ½" groove ¼" deep and ⅞" from the bottom edge on the inside face of each sliding block part. See the End View drawings, page 52, for location.

3. Glue and clamp the sliding-block pieces (A, B) together, with the bottom edges and ends flush. Repeat the gluing and clamping procedure with the two carriage parts (C).

4. After the glue dries, scrape the excess from the bottom edge of the sliding block and both edges of the carriage. Joint the edges if they are not flush. Now cut or rout a ½" dado ½" deep centered along the bottom edge of the sliding block where shown on the Sliding Block End View Drawing. (We used a ½" dado blade and cut the ½"-deep groove on the tablesaw.)

5. Crosscut the ends of the sliding block and carriage. The sliding block should be 12" long and the carriage 26" long.

6. Cut or rout a pair of ½" rabbets ⁷⁄₁₆" deep along the top edges of the carriage. Position the dadoed edge of the sliding block

on the rabbeted edge of the carriage. The sliding block should slide freely on the carriage with a minimum of free play. If the block doesn't slide easily, scrape or sand the rabbeted edges of the carriage where indicated on the Carriage End View Drawing.

Epoxy the hex nuts in position

1. Clamp the sliding block upright in a bench clamp. Now drill a ⅝" hole ⅜" deep *centered* over the ½ × ½" square hole into the end of the sliding block. (We used a Forstner bit.) If your drill-press table tilts, you could clamp the sliding block to the table, tilt the table, align the bit over the square hole, and drill the ⅝" hole. Repeat the process to drill a hole in the opposite end of the sliding block.

2. Push a ⅜" hex nut into one of the holes just drilled in the sliding block. From the opposite

end, insert a ⅜" hex nut into the other ⅝" hole. Thread the ⅜" all-thread rod through the sliding block, through the other hex nut, and about 2" or 3" past the second nut.

3. Once again, clamp the sliding block upright in a bench clamp. Mix a small amount of epoxy (we used quick-set). Being careful not to get any epoxy on the all-thread rod, epoxy the top ⅜" nut into the ⅝" hole. (We used a nail to fill the cavities around the nut with epoxy.) Immediately wipe off any excess epoxy. Later, after the epoxy has hardened, flip the assembly over, and epoxy the other nut into the opposite hole.

Add the end supports to the carriage

1. Cut the end supports (D) to the size listed in the Bill of Materials, page 52. *continued*

Accurate Box-Joint Jig

continued

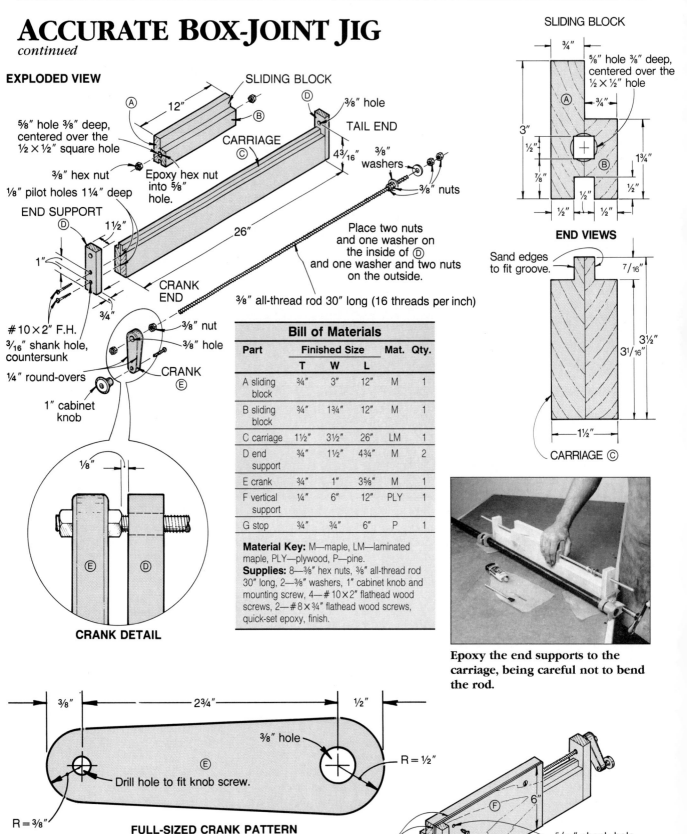

EXPLODED VIEW

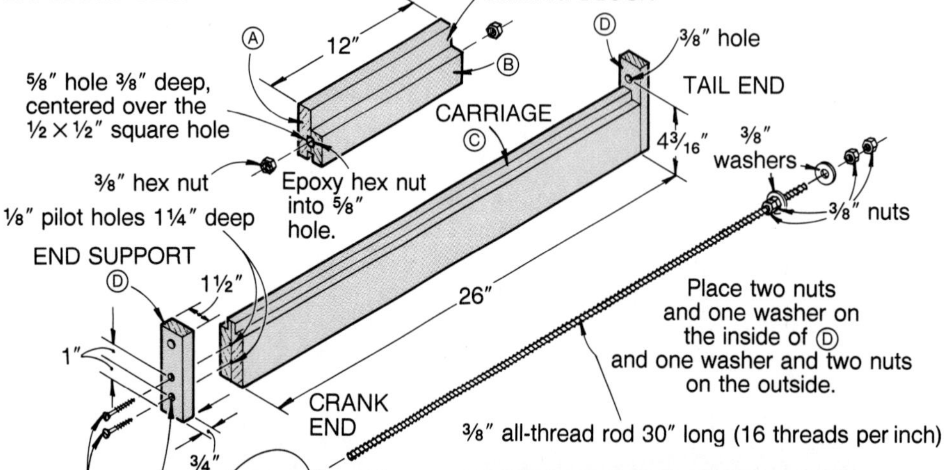

SLIDING BLOCK
A
12″
B
5/8″ hole 3/8″ deep, centered over the 1/2 × 1/2″ square hole
CARRIAGE
C
D
3/8″ hole
TAIL END
4 3/16″
3/8″ washers
3/8″ nuts
3/8″ hex nut
Epoxy hex nut into 5/8″ hole.
1/8″ pilot holes 1 1/4″ deep
END SUPPORT
D
1 1/2″
26″
Place two nuts and one washer on the inside of D and one washer and two nuts on the outside.
1″
CRANK END
3/8″ all-thread rod 30″ long (16 threads per inch)
3/4″

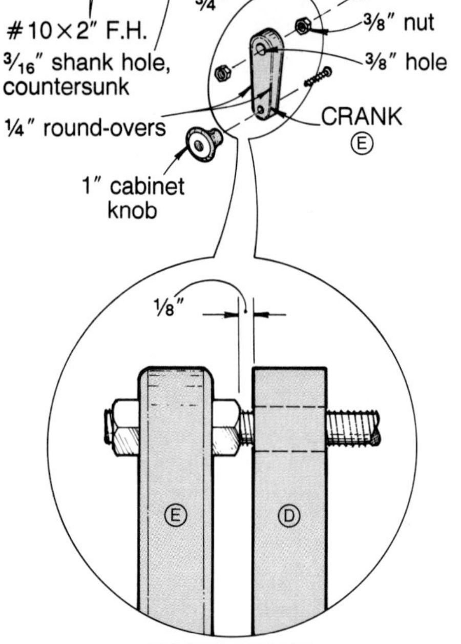

#10 × 2″ F.H.
3/16″ shank hole, countersunk
3/8″ nut
3/8″ hole
CRANK
E
1/4″ round-overs
1″ cabinet knob
1/8″
E
D

CRANK DETAIL

Bill of Materials					
Part	Finished Size			Mat.	Qty.
	T	W	L		
A sliding block	3/4″	3″	12″	M	1
B sliding block	3/4″	1 3/4″	12″	M	1
C carriage	1 1/2″	3 1/2″	26″	LM	1
D end support	3/4″	1 1/2″	4 3/4″	M	2
E crank	3/4″	1″	3 5/8″	M	1
F vertical support	1/4″	6″	12″	PLY	1
G stop	3/4″	3/4″	6″	P	1

Material Key: M—maple, LM—laminated maple, PLY—plywood, P—pine.
Supplies: 8—3/8″ hex nuts, 3/8″ all-thread rod 30″ long, 2—3/8″ washers, 1″ cabinet knob and mounting screw, 4—#10 × 2″ flathead wood screws, 2—#8 × 3/4″ flathead wood screws, quick-set epoxy, finish.

SLIDING BLOCK

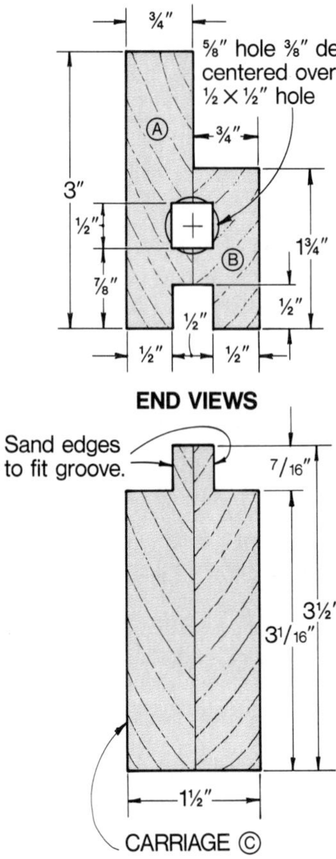

3/4″
5/8″ hole 3/8″ deep, centered over the 1/2 × 1/2″ hole
A
3/4″
3″
1/2″
B
1 3/4″
7/8″
1/2″
1/2″
1/2″
1/2″
Sand edges to fit groove.
7/16″
3 1/2″
3 1/16″
1 1/2″
CARRIAGE C

END VIEWS

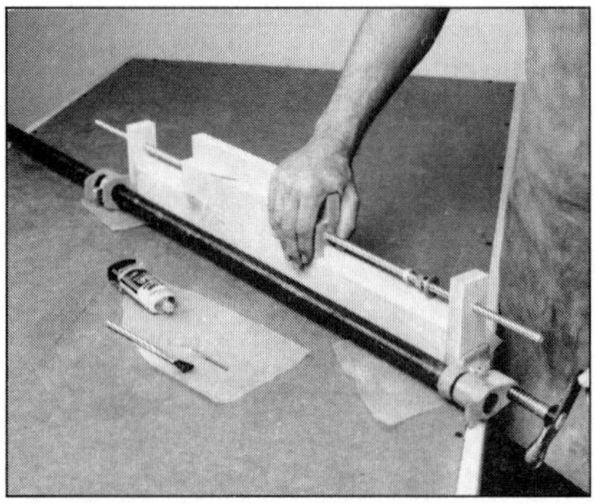

Epoxy the end supports to the carriage, being careful not to bend the rod.

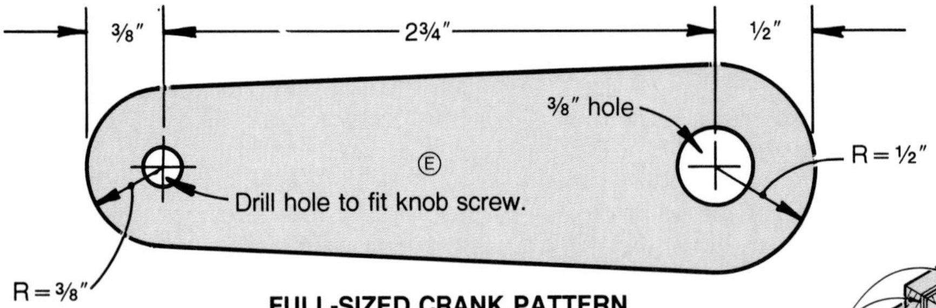

3/8″
2 3/4″
1/2″
3/8″ hole
E
R = 1/2″
Drill hole to fit knob screw.
R = 3/8″

FULL-SIZED CRANK PATTERN

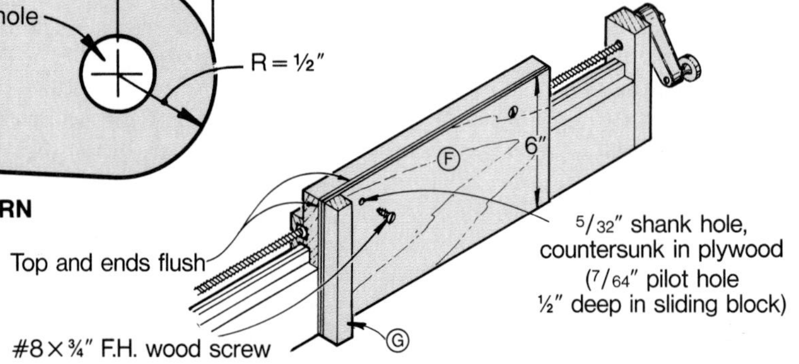

F
6″
Top and ends flush
5/32″ shank hole, countersunk in plywood (7/64″ pilot hole 1/2″ deep in sliding block)
#8 × 3/4″ F.H. wood screw
G

2. Mark the hole centerpoints, and drill a ⅜" hole through each end support where dimensioned on the Exploded View Drawing, *opposite.*

3. Thread two nuts and add a washer onto the tail end of the all-thread rod. As shown in the photo, *opposite,* slip an end support (D) onto each end of the rod and against the ends of the carriage. Epoxy and clamp the supports to the ends of the carriage. Position the end supports so the rod goes through the center of the hole in each support. Don't worry about the bottom end of the supports being perfectly flush with the carriage—just check that the rod remains straight.

4. Remove the clamps, drill the shank and pilot holes, and further secure each end support to the carriage with #10 × 2" wood screws. Sand the end supports flush with the carriage, and then finish-sand the entire assembly.

Make the crank

1. Using carbon paper, transfer the Full-Sized Crank Pattern and hole locations, *opposite,* to ¾" maple stock. Drill the holes where located, then cut the crank (E) to shape.

2. Rout a ¼" round-over on the crank edges where shown on the Exploded View Drawing. (To keep our fingers safely away from the router bit, we held the crank in a handscrew clamp as we routed the round-over on a table-mounted router.) Sand the crank smooth.

3. Double-nut the *tail* end of the rod to the end support. Position the nuts so the rod has no free play at the tail-end support, yet turns easily when rotated. (For tight-fitting joints later, you may need to adjust the nuts several times.)

4. Attach a cabinet knob to the crank. Next fasten the crank to the all-thread rod with two nuts. Leave a ⅛" gap between the inside nut and outside face of the end support where indicated on the Crank Detail, *opposite.*

Screw on the vertical support

To keep a long workpiece square with the saw table when cutting the joints, we found it necessary to add a vertical support (F) with a stop (G) to the sliding block. The vertical support also helps prevent excess chipping when cutting notches, so you might want to cut several vertical supports to replace the cut-up ones.

Build the vertical support (F, G) as shown on the drawing *opposite, bottom right,* and dimensioned in the Bill of Materials. Screw—*but do not glue*—the support to the carriage where shown on the drawing.

Using the Jig

Attach the jig to your miter gauge as shown and described on the three-step drawing, *below.*

When using the jig, remember that each crank revolution moves the sliding block ¹⁄₁₆". Always start with the crank in the down position. Attach the dado blade to the tablesaw, and raise the blade to the same height as the thickness of the piece being cut. Then raise the blade ¹⁄₃₂" higher so you can sand the fingers flush later. To start with a notch or a finger, follow steps 1 and 2 on the Starting with a Notch or Starting with a Finger drawing.

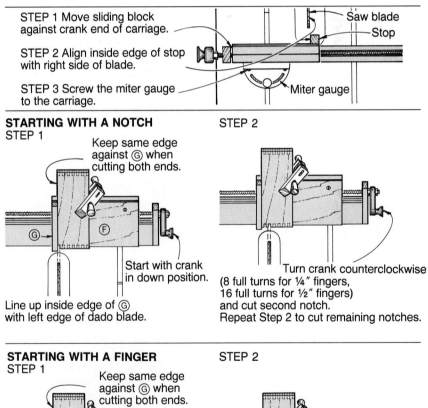

STEP 1 Move sliding block against crank end of carriage.

STEP 2 Align inside edge of stop with right side of blade.

STEP 3 Screw the miter gauge to the carriage.

Saw blade
Stop
Miter gauge

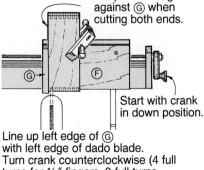

STARTING WITH A NOTCH
STEP 1
Keep same edge against ⒼG when cutting both ends.
Start with crank in down position.
Line up inside edge of ⒼG with left edge of dado blade.

STEP 2
Turn crank counterclockwise (8 full turns for ¼" fingers, 16 full turns for ½" fingers) and cut second notch.
Repeat Step 2 to cut remaining notches.

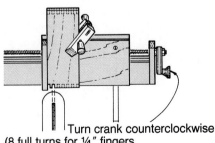

STARTING WITH A FINGER
STEP 1
Keep same edge against ⒼG when cutting both ends.
Start with crank in down position.
Line up left edge of ⒼG with left edge of dado blade. Turn crank counterclockwise (4 full turns for ¼" fingers, 8 full turns for ½" fingers) and make first cut.

STEP 2
Turn crank counterclockwise (8 full turns for ¼" fingers, 16 full turns for ½" fingers) and cut second notch.
Repeat Step 2 to cut remaining notches.

BACK-TO-BASICS SHOP LATHE

If you are considering buying a lathe, or even if you already have one, we invite you to take a close look at ours. It runs smoothly and quietly. The hefty bed, headstock, and tailstock, combined with the 1″ shafts, enable you to concentrate on turning without distracting vibrations. Although the idea of buying parts and assembling your own lathe may sound expensive, we found this lathe holds its own in our shop against commercial models costing twice as much.

Note: Since building this lathe, we've found a switch that works better than the one pictured here. It's listed in the Buying Guide on page 62. Also, you may prefer one of the commercial tool rests and bases discussed on page 63.

Start with the bed

1. Crosscut a 4×8′ sheet of ¾″ plywood (we used birch veneer) to 71″. Rip six strips (A) 7¾″ wide. Glue and clamp three pieces face-to-face for each *way* (horizontal bed member), with edges and ends flush.

2. After the glue dries, remove the·clamps and scrape off the excess glue from one edge of each way. Position the tablesaw rip fence 7⅝″ from the inside edge of the saw blade. Place the scraped edge against the fence, and with another person's help, trim the opposite edge smooth on each way. Reposition the fence 7½″ from the blade, and trim the opposite edge of each way. Crosscut one end of each way square, and then cut both to 70″.

3. With a helper and a dado blade mounted to the tablesaw, cut a 1³⁄₁₆″ stopped groove ⅝″ deep along the inside edge of each way where shown on the

Bed Assembly Drawing, *opposite.* (We marked the groove locations on each way before cutting to ensure a matching pair.) The grooves hold the sliding assembly for the tailstock and tool rest.

4. Cut eight ¾″ birch spacer pieces (B) to 3¾×11¾″ long. Glue and clamp two pairs of four pieces face-to-face to make two spacers. Following the same procedure as used to true up the ways, remove the glue and trim each spacer to 3½×11½″ long.

5. Mark and bore two ½″ holes through the top of each spacer, 3″ in from each end and centered from side to side. (See the Spacer Block Detail, *opposite.*)

6. Using the dimensions on the Bed Assembly Drawing, lay out

and mark the location of the eight ½″ holes on the front way. With a ½″ bit chucked into the drill press, bore the holes. Clamp the second way to the first face-to-face with the *top* edges and ends flush.

Using the holes in the front way as a guide, bore about ⅛″ into the second way. Unclamp the ways, go back to the drill press, and finish boring the ½″ holes through the second way. Position the spacers (one on each end) with the ends and bottoms flush with the ways; repeat this process to mark and bore three ⅝″ holes through each spacer.

7. Bolt the ways and spacers together. Using a square, check that the *top* edges of the ways are

BED ASSEMBLY

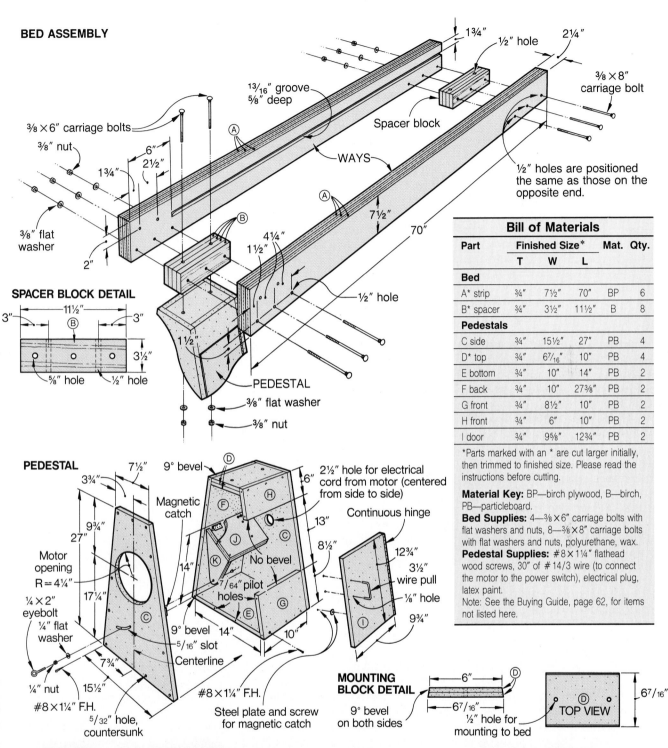

1¾"

½" hole

2¼"

3/8 × 8" carriage bolt

13/16" groove
5/8" deep

Spacer block

WAYS

3/8 × 6" carriage bolts

3/8" nut

1¾"

6"
2½"

½" holes are positioned
the same as those on the
opposite end.

A

3/8" flat
washer

2"

B

A

4¼"
1½"

7½"

70"

½" hole

SPACER BLOCK DETAIL

3"

11½"

3"

B

3½"

5/8" hole

½" hole

1½"

1½"

PEDESTAL

3/8" flat washer

3/8" nut

Bill of Materials

Part	Finished Size*			Mat.	Qty.
	T	W	L		
Bed					
A* strip	¾"	7½"	70"	BP	6
B* spacer	¾"	3½"	11½"	B	8
Pedestals					
C side	¾"	15½"	27"	PB	4
D* top	¾"	67/16"	10"	PB	4
E bottom	¾"	10"	14"	PB	2
F back	¾"	10"	273/8"	PB	2
G front	¾"	8½"	10"	PB	2
H front	¾"	6"	10"	PB	2
I door	¾"	95/8"	12¾"	PB	2

*Parts marked with an * are cut larger initially,
then trimmed to finished size. Please read the
instructions before cutting.

Material Key: BP—birch plywood, B—birch,
PB—particleboard.
Bed Supplies: 4—3/8 × 6" carriage bolts with
flat washers and nuts, 8—3/8 × 8" carriage bolts
with flat washers and nuts, polyurethane, wax.
Pedestal Supplies: #8 × 1¼" flathead
wood screws, 30" of #14/3 wire (to connect
the motor to the power switch), electrical plug,
latex paint.
Note: See the Buying Guide, page 62, for items
not listed here.

PEDESTAL

7½"

3¾"

9° bevel

D

2½" hole for electrical
cord from motor (centered
from side to side)

6"

9¾"

27"

Magnetic
catch

H

Continuous hinge

F

13"

Motor
opening
R = 4¼"

¼ × 2"
eyebolt
¼" flat
washer

17¼"

14"

J

K

No bevel

C

8½"

12¾"

3½"
wire pull

1/8" hole

9¾"

7/64" pilot
holes

E

G

C

I

¼" nut

7¾"

#8 × 1¼" F.H.

#8 × 1¼" F.H.

15½"

9° bevel

14"

10"

5/16" slot

Centerline

5/32" hole,
countersunk

Steel plate and screw
for magnetic catch

MOUNTING BLOCK DETAIL

6"

D

9° bevel
on both sides

67/16"

½" hole for
mounting to bed

D

TOP VIEW

67/16"

parallel and square as shown in
the photo at *left*. The oversized
holes in the ways and spacers
allow free play to align the ways.
Now remove the bolts. Glue and
rebolt the ways and spacers
together, again checking for
square. Belt-sand the top edges of
the ways smooth.

Construct the pedestals
*Note: The two pedestals are
identical except for the motor and
electrical cord cutouts in the
headstock pedestal.*

1. Cut four pieces of ¾"
particleboard to 15½ × 27" long.
Lay out one of the pedestal sides
(C) on one of the pieces, using
the dimensions on the *continued*

BACK-TO-BASICS SHOP LATHE
continued

Pedestal Drawing, page 55, as a guide. Using a straight board as a fence and a portable circular saw, cut the side piece to shape. Use this piece as a template to mark the other three sides, and then cut them to shape with the portable circular saw and fence.

2. Cut the motor opening in one of the sides and a cord-access hole in another (see the Pedestal Drawing for dimensions).

3. To make the 1½"-thick pedestal tops (D), start by cutting four pieces of ¾" particleboard to 7×11". Glue and clamp two pieces together face-to-face to make each top. Set your tablesaw blade 9° from center, and bevel-rip the two side edges to finished width (6⅞16"); crosscut to length (10") on the radial-arm saw (see Mounting Block Detail, page 55).

4. Cut the bottoms (E), backs (F), front parts (G, H), and doors (I) to the sizes listed in the Bill of Materials, page 55, bevel-cutting both ends of the bottoms and backs, the bottom edge of G, and the top edge of H at 9° where shown on the Pedestal Drawing.

5. Dry-clamp each pedestal together (minus the doors), and check the fit. Using the pilot- and shank-hole sizes stated on the Pedestal Drawing, drill and

countersink all the holes. Then glue, clamp, and screw each pedestal together. *Do not* glue the pedestal side with the motor hole in it. Screw it in place for now; you'll glue it in place later.

6. Drill the holes, and fasten a wire pull to each door. Cut two pieces of continuous (piano) hinge 12¾" long. Attach a hinge to each door, then mount the doors to the pedestals. Attach magnetic catches to the pedestals and steel plates to the doors.

Fashion the motor mount

1. Referring to the Motor Mount Drawing, *opposite,* cut the top piece (J) to size. Drill the ¼" holes and mount the hinges to the top piece.

2. To make the vertical support (K), cut a piece of ¾" plywood to 7½" square. Draw a diagonal line from corner to corner, and cut along the line to cut the piece in two. On one of the pieces, lay out the ⁵⁄16" hole and ¾" radius on the support. Cut the radius to shape and drill the hole. Glue and screw the top piece to the support.

3. Working inside the motor pedestal, measure up 14" from the top of the base (E), and make a mark across the back piece (F)

where shown on the Pedestal Drawing on page 55. Hold the motor mount so the top face of (J) aligns with the marked line and against the left-hand side (C). Mark the location of the hinge holes on the back piece, remove the motor mount, drill the holes, and bolt the motor mount to the back piece.

Attach the bed

1. Position the pedestals about 4' apart. Lay the bed assembly on top of the two pedestals. Reposition the pedestals so the ends of the bed are flush with the outside face of each pedestal.

2. Using the previously bored holes in each spacer (B) as guides, bore two ½"-diameter holes through the top of each pedestal. Bolt the bed to the pedestals.

Laminate and machine the headstock

Note: We give a source for the spindles in the Buying Guide on page 62. If you wish to have them made locally, take the spindle drawings opposite *and on page 59 to a machinist. You need both spindles to continue construction.*

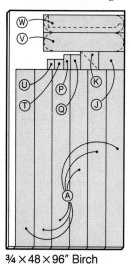

¾ × 48 × 96″ Birch Plywood

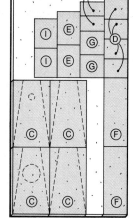

¾ × 48 × 96″ Particleboard

Cutting Diagram

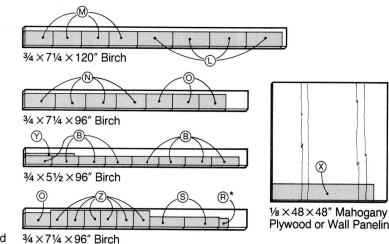

¾ × 7¼ × 120″ Birch

¾ × 7¼ × 96″ Birch

¾ × 5½ × 96″ Birch

¾ × 7¼ × 96″ Birch
*Plane or resaw Ⓡ to ½″.

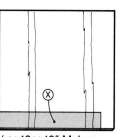

⅛ × 48 × 48″ Mahogany Plywood or Wall Paneling

MOTOR MOUNT

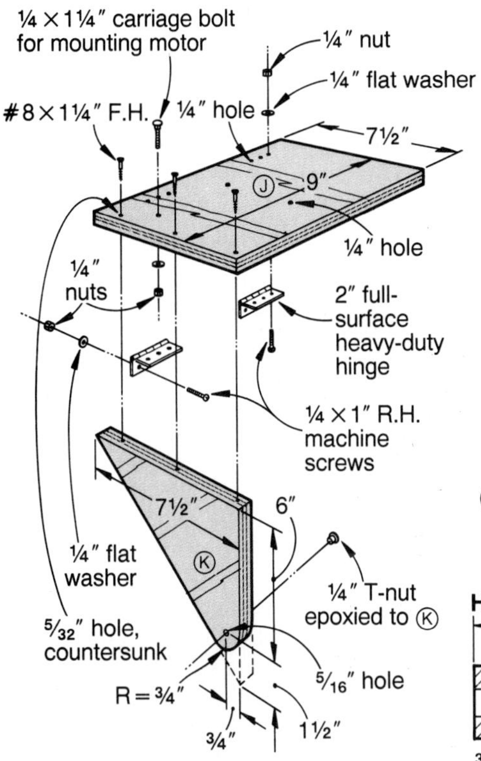

¼ × 1¼″ carriage bolt for mounting motor
¼″ nut
¼″ flat washer
#8 × 1¼″ F.H.
¼″ hole
7½″
J
9″
¼″ hole
¼″ nuts
2″ full-surface heavy-duty hinge
¼ × 1″ R.H. machine screws
7½″
6″
K
¼″ flat washer
¼″ T-nut epoxied to K
5/32″ hole, countersunk
5/16″ hole
R = ¾″
¾″
1½″

HEADSTOCK

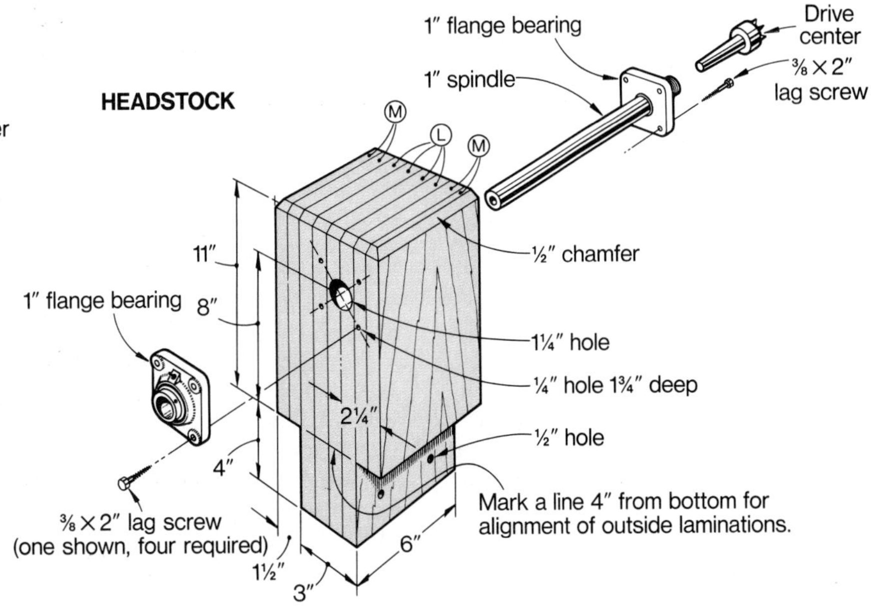

1″ flange bearing
Drive center
1″ spindle
⅜ × 2″ lag screw
M
L
M
½″ chamfer
11″
1″ flange bearing
8″
1¼″ hole
¼″ hole 1¾″ deep
2¼″
½″ hole
4″
Mark a line 4″ from bottom for alignment of outside laminations.
⅜ × 2″ lag screw (one shown, four required)
1½″
6″
3″

HEADSTOCK SPINDLE

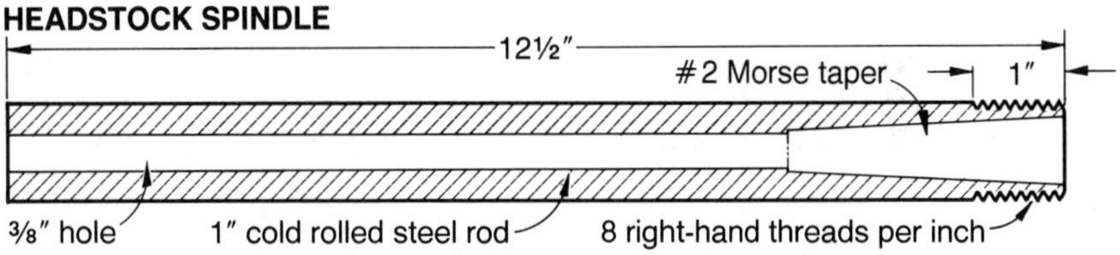

12½″
#2 Morse taper
1″
⅜″ hole
1″ cold rolled steel rod
8 right-hand threads per inch

Bill of Materials

Part	Finished Size*			Mat.	Qty.
	T	W	L		
Motor Mount					
J top	¾″	9″	7½″	BP	1
K* support	¾″	7½″	6¾″	BP	1

*Part marked with an * is cut larger initially, then trimmed to finished size. Please read the instructions before cutting.

Material Key: BP—birch plywood.
Motor Mount Supplies: #8 × 1¼″ flathead wood screws, 1 pair—2″ full-surface heavy-duty hinges, ¼ × 1″ roundhead machine screws with flat washers and nuts, ¼ × 2″ eyebolt with nut and washer and T-nut, 4—¼ × 1¼″ carriage bolts with nuts and washers for mounting motor.

Bill of Materials

Part	Finished Size*			Mat.	Qty.
	T	W	L		
Headstock					
L* middle section	¾″	6″	15″	B	4
M* outer section	¾″	6″	11″	B	4

*Parts marked with an * are cut larger initially, then trimmed to finished size. Please read the instructions before cutting.

Material Key: B—birch.
Headstock Supplies: 8—⅜ × 2″ lag screws, ¼″ steel rod 16″ long for knocking centers out of spindles, clear polyurethane.

CENTERING DETAIL

Mark diagonals through centerpoint with a combination square.

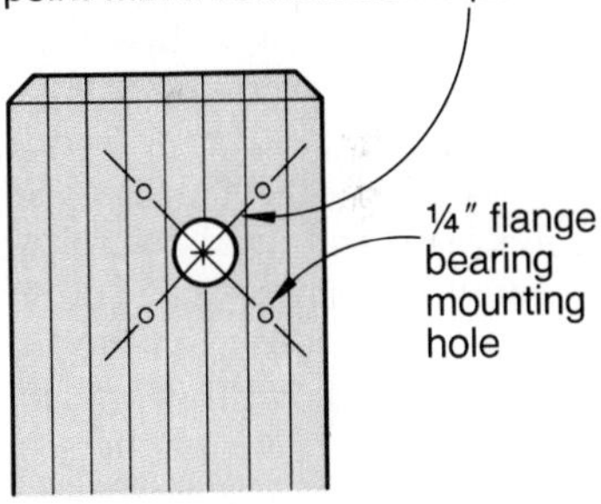

¼″ flange bearing mounting hole

1. Cut four pieces of ¾″ birch to 6¼ × 15½″ long for the middle section of the headstock (L). Glue and clamp the pieces together with the edges and ends flush. Again, following the same procedure used to true up the ways, remove the excess glue and trim the lamination to 6 × 15″.

2. Check the fit of the lamination between the ways; sand the bottom 4″ if necessary for a snug fit.

3. Cut four pieces of ¾″ birch to 6¼ × 11½″ for the outer sections (M). Glue two pieces of birch face-to-face for each outer section. Rip and crosscut each lamination to 6 × 11″.

4. Sandwich the middle lamination (L) between the two outer laminations (M). The bottom of the middle lamination should extend exactly 4″ farther than the bottoms of the two outer laminations. Apply glue to the mating surfaces, carefully align the edges, and clamp the headstock together. Later, remove excess glue; belt-sand smooth.

5. Position the headstock between the ways, flush with the end of the bed. Using the two previously bored ½″ holes in the front way as guides, bore about ⅛″ into the headstock to mark the hole locations. Remove the headstock and use a drill press to finish boring through it.

6. Using the dimensions on the Headstock Drawing, *above,* as a guide, mark the location of the

continued

BACK-TO-BASICS SHOP LATHE
continued

spindle hole on the headstock. Use a combination square to mark diagonal lines like those shown on the Centering Detail, page 57. (You'll use the diagonals to align the flange bearings later.) With a drill press, bore a 1¼" hole *completely* through the headstock (we used a spade bit to bore as deep as possible, then added a bit extension to finish boring the hole). Again, using a combination square, mark diagonals centered on the 1¼" hole on the opposite end of the headstock.

7. Rout a ½" chamfer along the top edges of the headstock.

8. Bolt and glue the headstock to the bed assembly. Slip one bearing onto the headstock spindle, insert the spindle through the 1¼" hole in the headstock, and slide the other bearing in position on the opposite end. Using the diagonals marked earlier, center the bearings over the 1¼" hole on the headstock, and mark the location of the bearing mounting holes. Remove the bearings and spindle from the headstock, and drill the mounting holes. Screw the bearing-spindle assembly to the headstock. Lock the spindle in position so that 1⅛" of the threaded end of the spindle extend beyond the inboard edge of the headstock. (See the Buying Guide, page 62, for a source for these items.)

Build and assemble the tailstock

1. Cut four pieces of ¾" birch to 6¼ × 13" to form the middle lamination (N). Cut or rout a ½" groove ½" deep, centered from edge to edge, the length of one of

the pieces. Glue and clamp the four pieces together face-to-face, with the grooved piece in position where shown on the Tailstock Drawing, *opposite.* Later, remove the excess glue, and trim to 6 × 12½", following the same procedure used to true up the ways.

2. Check the fit of the middle section between the ways. If necessary, belt-sand the bottom 1½" so the bottom of the lamination slides easily between the ways (be careful not to sand above the 1½" mark).

3. Cut four pieces 6¼ × 11½" from ¾" birch for the two outer laminated sections (O). Glue two sets of two pieces together face-to-face. Rip and crosscut each outer lamination to 6 × 11" long.

4. Sandwich the middle lamination between the two outer laminations, and repeat the procedure in step 4 of the headstock lamination, positioning the bottom of the center lamination 1½" below the bottom edges of the two outer laminations. Later, remove the excess glue from the tailstock, belt-sand smooth, and rout the chamfer on the top edges.

5. Cut the sliding assembly (P, Q) to the sizes listed in the Bill of Materials and shown on the Tailstock Slider Detail, *opposite.* With the ends flush, position the smaller piece (P), centered from side to side, on the larger piece (Q), and glue and screw it in position. Then cut the spindle positioner (R) to size from ½" birch. Draw diagonals and bore a 1" hole through the center of the positioner.

6. Position the tailstock between the ways on the lathe. Slide and center the sliding assembly (P, Q) directly under the tailstock. Insert a ⅜ × 16" threaded rod through the ½" groove in the tailstock, and mark its position on the sliding

assembly. Remove the sliding assembly, drill a ⁷⁄₁₆" hole through it where marked, and epoxy a ⅜" T-nut in the hole on the bottom side. Slide the assembly back in position under the tailstock, and using a nut and washer on the top of the threaded rod, bolt the tailstock and assembly together.

7. To mark the position of the spindle hole on the tailstock, start by positioning a drive center in the spindle mounted in the *headstock.* Slide the tailstock against the headstock spindle until the drive center leaves a small depression in the tailstock. Remove the tailstock and bore a 1⅝" hole ¾" deep where indented (we used a Forstner bit). Switch to a 1¼" bit, center in the 1⅝" hole, and bore a hole completely through the tailstock.

8. Thread a 1" nut onto the end of the tailstock spindle, and wrap tape around the spindle near its midsection to center the spindle in the 1¼" hole where shown on the Tailstock Section Drawing, *opposite.* Lay the tailstock on its side so the spindle stands vertically and the nut faces up. Center, then epoxy the nut in the 1⅝" hole by filling the voids around the perimeter of the nut with sawdust-thickened epoxy. After the epoxy has hardened, turn the tailstock over, and drill mounting holes for the spindle positioner (R) on the side opposite the 1" nut. Remove the spindle from the tailstock, and remove the tape from the spindle.

9. To make the spindle lock assembly, start by drilling a ⅜" hole ½" deep into the side of the tailstock where shown on the tailstock drawings. Then drill a ⁵⁄₁₆" hole through the center of the ⅜" hole that reaches the 1¼" spindle hole. Screw a ¼" threaded insert into the ⅜" hole. Saw off the head of a ¼ × 4" carriage bolt. Then, halfway along its length, bend it at a 90° angle.

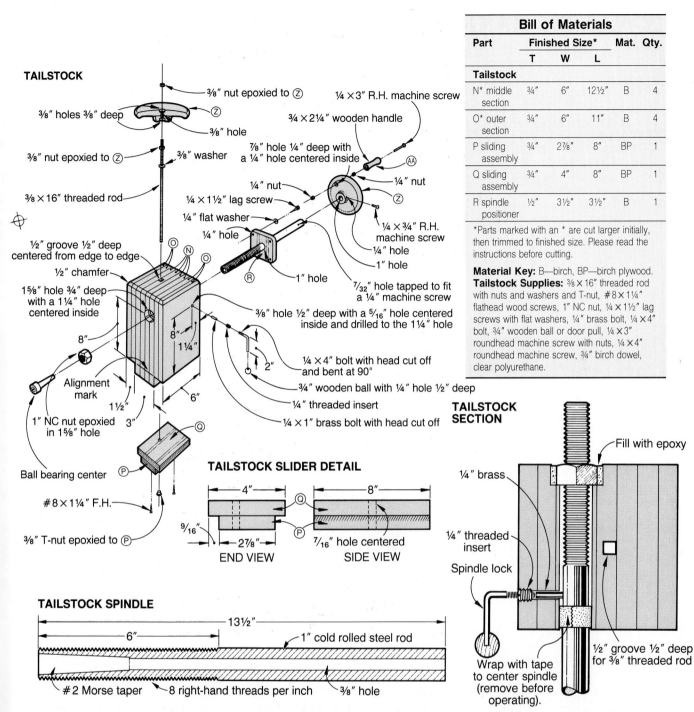

TAILSTOCK

⅜" nut epoxied to Ⓩ

¼ × 3" R.H. machine screw

⅜" holes ⅜" deep

Ⓩ

¾ × 2¼" wooden handle

⅜" hole

⅞" hole ¼" deep with a ¼" hole centered inside

⅜" nut epoxied to Ⓩ

⅜" washer

ⒶⒶ

¼" nut

⅜ × 16" threaded rod

¼ × 1½" lag screw

¼" nut

Ⓩ

¼" flat washer

¼ × ¾" R.H. machine screw

¼" nut

¼" hole

1" hole

½" groove ½" deep centered from edge to edge

Ⓞ

Ⓝ

Ⓞ

¼" hole

½" chamfer

Ⓡ

1" hole

7/32" hole tapped to fit a ¼" machine screw

1⅝" hole ¾" deep with a 1¼" hole centered inside

8"

8"

1¼"

⅜" hole ½" deep with a 5/16" hole centered inside and drilled to the 1¼" hole

8"

1½"

6"

¼ × 4" bolt with head cut off and bent at 90°

Alignment mark

¾" wooden ball with ¼" hole ½" deep

1" NC nut epoxied in 1⅝" hole

3"

¼" threaded insert

¼ × 1" brass bolt with head cut off

Ball bearing center

Ⓟ

Ⓠ

#8 × 1¼" F.H.

⅜" T-nut epoxied to Ⓟ

TAILSTOCK SLIDER DETAIL

4"

Ⓠ

8"

9/16"

2⅞"

Ⓟ

7/16" hole centered

END VIEW

SIDE VIEW

TAILSTOCK SPINDLE

13½"

6"

1" cold rolled steel rod

#2 Morse taper

8 right-hand threads per inch

⅜" hole

Bill of Materials

Part	Finished Size*			Mat.	Qty.
	T	W	L		
Tailstock					
N* middle section	¾"	6"	12½"	B	4
O* outer section	¾"	6"	11"	B	4
P sliding assembly	¾"	2⅞"	8"	BP	1
Q sliding assembly	¾"	4"	8"	BP	1
R spindle positioner	½"	3½"	3½"	B	1

*Parts marked with an * are cut larger initially, then trimmed to finished size. Please read the instructions before cutting.

Material Key: B—birch, BP—birch plywood.
Tailstock Supplies: ⅜ × 16" threaded rod with nuts and washers and T-nut, #8 × 1¼" flathead wood screws, 1" NC nut, ¼ × 1½" lag screws with flat washers, ¼" brass bolt, ¼ × 4" bolt, ¾" wooden ball or door pull, ¼ × 3" roundhead machine screw with nuts, ¼ × 4" roundhead machine screw, ¾" birch dowel, clear polyurethane.

TAILSTOCK SECTION

Fill with epoxy

¼" brass

¼" threaded insert

Spindle lock

Wrap with tape to center spindle (remove before operating).

½" groove ½" deep for ⅜" threaded rod

Drill a ¼" hole ½" deep in a wooden ball or round door pull, and epoxy it to the non-threaded end of the bolt.

10. Cut the head off a ¼ × 1" brass bolt (brass will not damage the tailstock spindle when tightening the spindle lock later). Working inside the 1¼" hole in the tailstock, insert the brass bolt into the 5/16" hole with needle-nose pliers. Attach the positioner.

Make the belt guard

1. Cut two pieces of ¾" birch plywood to 7 × 33½" for the belt-guard sides (V, W). Mark a 3½" radius on both ends of one piece, and using double-faced tape, tape it to the bottom of the other piece. Cut the two pieces to shape, sand the cut edges smooth, pry apart, and remove the tape.

2. Mark the location, then cut the notched portion of W to shape, using the dimensions on the Belt Guard Drawing, page 60.

3. Bore a 1" hole through V where marked. (The 1" access hole allows you to drive a knock-out rod through the headstock spindle to remove the drive center when changing to a faceplate.) *continued*

BACK-TO-BASICS SHOP LATHE
continued

BELT GUARD

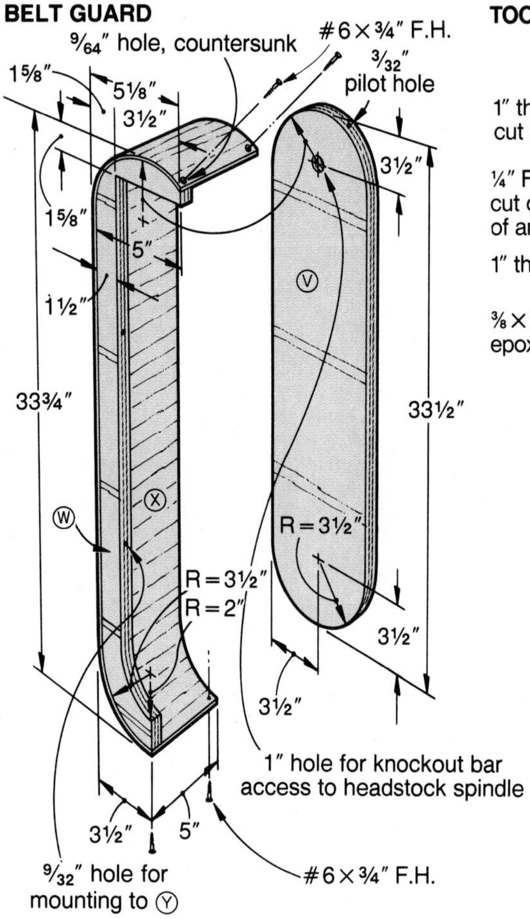

9/64" hole, countersunk
#6 × 3/4" F.H.
3/32" pilot hole
1 5/8"
5 1/8"
3 1/2"
3 1/2"
1 5/8"
5"
1 1/2"
V
33 3/4"
33 1/2"
W
X
R = 3 1/2"
R = 3 1/2"
R = 2"
3 1/2"
3 1/2"
1" hole for knockout bar access to headstock spindle
3 1/2"
5"
9/32" hole for mounting to Y
#6 × 3/4" F.H.

TOOL REST

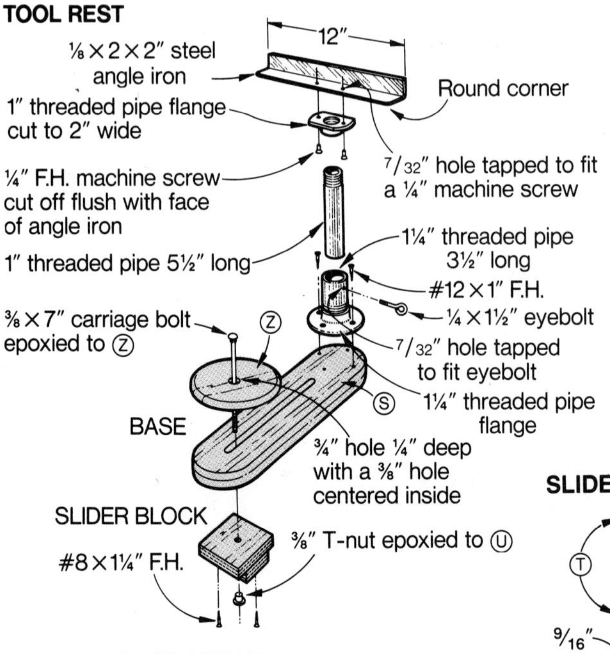

12"
1/8 × 2 × 2" steel angle iron
Round corner
1" threaded pipe flange cut to 2" wide
7/32" hole tapped to fit a 1/4" machine screw
1/4" F.H. machine screw cut off flush with face of angle iron
1 1/4" threaded pipe 3 1/2" long
1" threaded pipe 5 1/2" long
#12 × 1" F.H.
1/4 × 1 1/2" eyebolt
3/8 × 7" carriage bolt epoxied to Z
Z
7/32" hole tapped to fit eyebolt
S
1 1/4" threaded pipe flange
BASE
3/4" hole 1/4" deep with a 3/8" hole centered inside
SLIDER BLOCK
#8 × 1 1/4" F.H.
3/8" T-nut epoxied to U

SLIDER BLOCK DETAIL

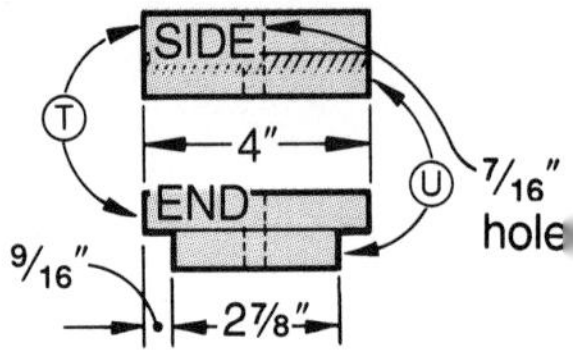

SIDE
T
4"
END
U
7/16" hole
9/16"
2 7/8"

BASE DETAIL

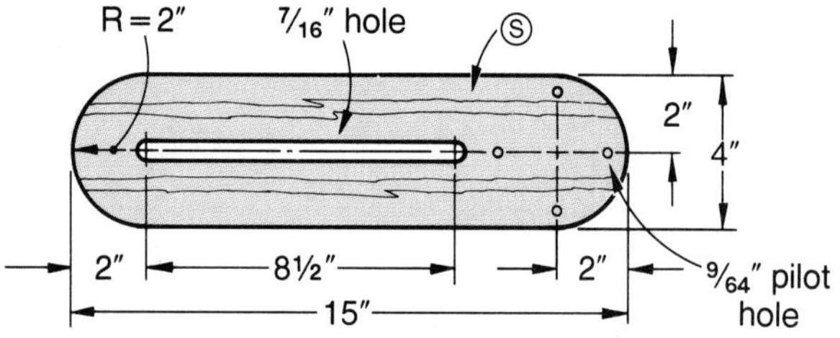

R = 2"
7/16" hole
S
2"
4"
2"
8 1/2"
2"
15"
9/64" pilot hole

Bill of Materials					
Part	Finished Size T	W	L	Mat.	Qty.
Belt Guard					
V side	3/4"	33 1/2"	7"	BP	1
W side	3/4"	33 1/2"	5"	BP	1
X wrap-around	1/8"	39 1/2"	5"	MP	1
Y mounting strip	3/4"	3/4"	20"	B	1

Material Key: BP—birch plywood, MP—mahogany plywood, B—birch.
Belt Guard Supplies: #6 × 3/4" flathead wood screws, #8 × 1 1/4" flathead wood screws, 2—1/4 × 1 3/4" carriage bolts with washers and wing nuts, latex paint.

Bill of Materials					
Part	Finished Size T	W	L	Mat.	Qty.
Tool Rest					
S base	1 1/2"	4"	15"	LB	1
T sliding assembly	3/4"	4"	4"	BP	1
U sliding assembly	3/4"	2 7/8"	4"	BP	1

Material Key: LB—laminated birch, BP—birch plywood.
Tool Rest Supplies: 1/8 × 2 × 12" steel angle iron, 1/4 × 1/2" flathead machine screws, 1" threaded pipe flange, 1 1/4" threaded pipe flange, 1 × 5 1/2" threaded pipe, 1 1/4 × 3 1/2" threaded pipe, 1/4 × 1 1/2" eyebolt, 3/8 × 7" carriage bolt with 3/8" T-nut, #12 × 1" flathead wood screws, #8 × 1 1/4" flathead wood screws, clear polyurethane, enamel paint.

4. Rip and crosscut the wraparound piece (X) to size from 1/8" plywood or wall paneling. To make the plywood flexible, soak it in hot water. (We soaked ours in a bathtub for more than an hour.) Wrap the plywood around the side pieces (V, W), clamp it in position with band clamps, and let dry. (It is important to have the wraparound piece clamped while it dries so it will maintain its curved shape when dry. Also, do not glue and screw until the wraparound has dried thoroughly; otherwise, the glue won't stick to it.) Then drill pilot holes, and glue and screw the wraparound to the two belt-guard side pieces.

5. Cut the mounting strip (Y) to finished size.

Building the tool rest

Using the dimensions on the Tool Rest Drawing and the two detail drawings, *opposite,* cut the parts to size and build the tool rest. (We cut the metal parts with a hacksaw and tapped the holes.) Make the tool-rest base (S) out of laminated material for strength, and make it plenty long for sufficient reach when turning large-diameter bowls.

Rotating the handwheel (which we explain how to build later) loosens or tightens the sliding assembly (T, U) in the grooves in the bed. This allows you to position the tool rest where desired, and then fasten it firmly in place.

Assemble the lathe

1. Buy a 30" length of #14/3 electrical cable, and wire one end to the motor so the motor rotates in the direction shown on the Final Assembly Drawing at *right.* Wire a 3-pronged (grounded) plug to the other end of the electrical cable.

2. Attach the 1" step pulley to the headstock spindle and the 5/8" step pulley to the motor. Tighten the setscrews on each pulley. Clamp the motor to the motor mount and add the belt. Adjust the position of the motor so the pulleys align. Mark the motor hole locations on the motor mount, remove the motor, and drill the holes to size. Bolt the motor to the motor mount with carriage bolts, and tighten securely.

3. To form the 5/16" motor adjustment slot, start by moving the motor mount to its highest position. Stick a pencil through the hole in part K, and move the motor mount and the motor up and down to scribe the slot. Remove the marked pedestal side (C) from the pedestal assembly, and drill a 5/16" hole at each end of the marked slot. Now cut the arc-shaped slot with a jigsaw. Position the pedestal side against the pedestal assembly, and check the slot in the pedestal side against the hole in K. Trim if

necessary, and then glue and screw the pedestal side to the pedestal. Epoxy the T-nut to the motor mount (see the Motor Mount Drawing, page 57) and add the 1/4 × 2" eyebolt.

4. Run the belt from the motor pulley to the headstock pulley. Push down slightly on the motor to tighten the belt, and tighten the 1/4" eyebolt on the outside of the pedestal to hold the motor mount in position.

5. Mount the power switch on the front way above the motor pedestal. Plug the motor cord into the outlet in the power switch.

6. Remove or mask off all the hardware. Sand all the wooden parts smooth. Paint the pedestals, belt guard, and metal tool-rest parts. Apply clear polyurethane to the bed assembly, headstock,

tailstock, and tool-rest base. Later, remove the masking or reattach the hardware; apply wax to the groove in each way so the slide assemblies will slide easily.

7. To attach the belt guard to the lathe, start by drilling 9/32" holes and bolting the mounting strip (Y) to the guard (V, W, X). Then position the assembly over the pulleys and belts. Working from the back side, mark the location of the mounting strip on the lathe, and drill mounting holes in the lathe. Finally, separate the guard from the strip, screw the strip to the lathe, and bolt the guard to the lathe.

Turn the handwheels using your new lathe

1. Assemble the lathe as directed (don't forget the belt guard). *continued*

FINAL ASSEMBLY

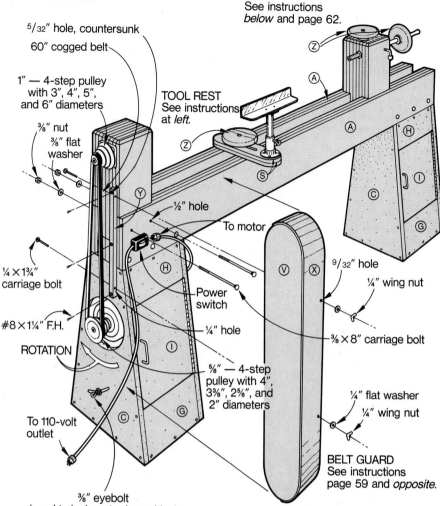

5/32" hole, countersunk

60" cogged belt

1" — 4-step pulley with 3", 4", 5", and 6" diameters

3/8" nut

3/8" flat washer

TOOL REST See instructions at *left.*

HANDWHEELS See instructions *below* and page 62.

1/4 × 1¾" carriage bolt

½" hole

To motor

#8 × 1¼" F.H.

ROTATION

Power switch

1/4" hole

9/32" hole

1/4" wing nut

3/8 × 8" carriage bolt

5/8" — 4-step pulley with 4", 3⅜", 2⅝", and 2" diameters

1/4" flat washer

1/4" wing nut

BELT GUARD See instructions page 59 and *opposite.*

To 110-volt outlet

3/8" eyebolt (used to lock motor in position)

61

BACK-TO-BASICS SHOP LATHE
continued

HANDWHEELS

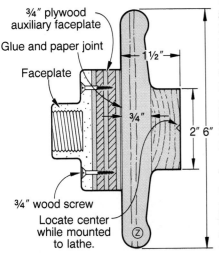

¾" plywood
auxiliary faceplate

Glue and paper joint

Faceplate

1½"

¾"

2" 6"

¾" wood screw

Locate center
while mounted
to lathe.

Z

TAILSTOCK HANDLE

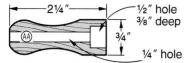

2¼"

½" hole
⅜" deep

¾"

¼" hole

AA

Bill of Materials

Part	Finished Size*			Mat.	Qty.
	T	W	L		
Handwheels					
Z* hand-wheel	1½"	6" diam.		LB	3
AA tailstock handle	¾" diam.		2¼"	BD	1

*Part marked with an * is cut larger initially, then trimmed to finished size. Please read the instructions before cutting.

Material Key: LB—laminated birch, BD—birch dowel.

For now, fasten the tool rest to the bed with a bolt and washer. Position the belt on the steps closest to the motor and headstock (575 rpm).

2. Cut six pieces of ¾" birch to 7×7" for the handwheels (Z). Laminate two pieces face-to-face to form each handwheel blank. Draw diagonals to find center, and scribe a 6¼"-diameter circle on each blank. Bandsaw each to rough circular shape.

3. Glue and clamp a birch blank to an auxiliary faceplate

using a paper and glue joint as shown on the Handwheels Drawing at *left*. Turn the handwheel to shape on your new lathe, sand smooth, and mark the centerpoint. Separate the handwheel from the faceplate by prying the two apart at the glue joint with a chisel. Repeat step 3 to make the other two handwheels.

4. Using the dimensions on the Tailstock Drawing, page 59, drill the holes at the marked center-point for mounting one handwheel to the tailstock spindle and one to the top of the tailstock. Drill the mounting holes in the third handwheel, using the dimensions on the Tool Rest Drawing, page 60.

5. Mount a handwheel to the tailstock spindle, drill a ¼" hole through the handwheel, then drill a 7/32" hole into the spindle. Remove the handwheel and thread the hole in the spindle with a ¼" tap. Insert a ¼" roundhead machine screw through the ¼" hole, and fasten the handwheel to the spindle. Drill the mounting holes for the wooden handle (AA) in the tailstock-spindle handwheel (see the Tailstock Drawing for hole dimensions). Finish all three handwheels, then mount the other two.

6. To form the tailstock handle (AA), first cut a piece of ¾" birch dowel 2¼" long. Using a drill press, drill the holes shown on the Tailstock Handle Drawing, *above left*. Turn the handle to shape between centers, then mount it to the handwheel on the tailstock spindle.

Using the lathe

Add sand to the bottom of each pedestal to minimize vibration. To move the tailstock and tool rest, loosen by turning their handwheels counterclockwise. Move them to the desired

SPEED CHART

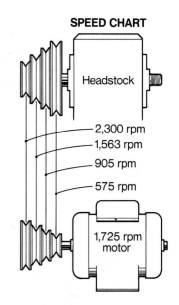

Headstock

2,300 rpm
1,563 rpm
905 rpm
575 rpm

1,725 rpm
motor

position, and turn the handwheels clockwise to lock.

The chart *above* shows the speeds available using the step pulleys. Try the slowest speed until you're used to the lathe.

Buying Guide
• **Headstock and tailstock spindles, flange bearings, and pulleys.** Spindles, cold-rolled steel, fully machined and ready for mounting. 1" flange bearings with locking collars. 1" 4-step pulley (sheave), ⅝" 4-step pulley, 60" cogged belt. Northwest Carving Supplies, P.O. Box 407, 123 W. Railroad Ave. N, Manhattan, MT 59741. Call 406/284-6009.
• **Spindle attachments.** Drive center (for headstock), catalog no. 46-933. Ball-bearing center (for tailstock), catalog no. 465302. 3" faceplate, catalog no. 46-936. 6" faceplate, catalog no. 46-937. For current prices, contact Puckett Electric Tools, 841 Eleventh St., Des Moines, IA 50309, or call 800-544-4189 or 515/244-4189.
• **Power switch.** Catalog no. A526. Contact AMT, P.O. Box 70, Royersford, PA 19468, or call 215/948-0400, for current price.

Making a Good Lathe Even Better

Since we built the lathe featured on the preceding pages, several *WOOD*® magazine staffers have constructed models for their personal shops. And, according to our suppliers, more than 300 readers have ordered the parts to build their own.

After many hours of use, we found our homemade tool rest wasn't as easy to use as most commercial models. Striving for improvement, we ordered several tool rests and bases and tried them on our lathe.

Which is the best? It's hard to say. Each performed well (admittedly better than our homemade version), so we decided to show you the four we tested, and let you choose the best system for your needs.

We added ½ × 2½ × 64″ steel strips to the top of the ways for three of the bases to track on. The steel and cutting cost us $25 at a local machine shop. The fourth base, made by Conover Woodcraft Specialties, tracks on the wooden ways of the lathe as designed. The drawing *below* shows the steel strips screwed to the laminated-plywood ways.

Pick the tool rest and base that best fit your needs

Of the four models we tested, we found that the easiest on the pocketbook was the Rockwell

END SECTION

Dimension of gap depends on the base you choose.

#14 × 2″ F.H. wood screws spaced every 6″

¼″ hole, countersunk
¼″ shank hole ½″ deep
5/32″ pilot hole 1⅛″ deep
½ × 2½″ steel bar stock
Lathe ways

standard base (no. 46-831), *below*. Both this unit and the deluxe Rockwell base shown at *bottom*, require a custom-made height-adjustment adapter from Puckett Electric Tools (see below). Both the 12″-long rest (no. 46-692) and the 4″-long rest (no. 46-690) are strong, with a 1″-diameter shaft. For bowl turning, consider an outside French curl rest (46-404).

The gap between the steel strips measures 1⅝″ for both this base and the deluxe model. For current prices, contact Puckett Electric Tools, 841 Eleventh St., Des Moines, IA 50309, or call 800-544-4189 or 515/244-4189.

Rockwell standard tool-rest base

Sturdier and more expensive, the Rockwell deluxe tool-rest base (no. 46-171) shown *below* holds the same rests as those mentioned for the standard base. Contact Puckett Electric Tools (address above) for information on current prices.

Rockwell deluxe tool-rest base

Bowl turners will love General's extended base (no. 2614). Its 13½″ length makes reaching the outside of a large bowl a breeze. The standard tool-rest base (no. 164) measures 9¼″ long. The S-curve bowl rest (no. BR500) shown *below* makes turning the curved surfaces of bowls easier with less chatter. The rest allows you to support your turning tool next to the curved surface. The gap between the steel strips measures 1⅞″. For current prices, contact Sisco Supply, 102 Kimball Ave., South Burlington, VT 05403, or call 802/863-9036.

General extended tool-rest base

The Conover base shown *below* mounts to the ways without adding the steel strips. (Our lathe already had the strips attached before we took the picture.) The base (CL16-300) tightens to the ways by the use of a handwheel located below the ways. Two rests are available: the 12″ rest shown (CL16-306-12) and a 6″ rest (CL16-307). For current prices, contact Conover Woodcraft Specialties, 18125 Madison Rd., Parkman, OH 44080; call 216/548-3481.

Conover tool-rest base

DRUM-SANDING TABLE

Whether you sand curves without the fence or edge-sand with the fence, you'll find our drum-sanding table pleasurably clean and easy to use.

This dust-collecting drum-sanding table not only keeps your shop cleaner, but its offset fence also allows you to edge-sand stock. With the fence in place, simply feed stock slowly into the rotating sanding drum mounted in your drill press. The slight offset we designed into the fence lets you edge-sand stock to $\frac{1}{32}''$ precision. (P.S. Removable inserts make switching to different-sized sanding drums a snap.)

Construct the sanding table

1. Cut the tabletop (A) to the size listed in the Bill of Materials. Mark the corner radii with a compass, and cut the corners to shape. Sand, but don't round over, the tabletop edges.

2. Cut two pieces of plastic laminate to cover the top and bottom of the tabletop, allowing 1″ in both directions for overlap. Apply the laminate to the top of the tabletop with contact cement. Using a router with a flush-trim bit, rout the laminate flush. Repeat this procedure with the laminate on the bottom of the tabletop.

3. Mark the location of the square insert hole on the tabletop where shown in the Exploded View Drawing, *opposite*. Drill a 1″ hole inside the outline in each corner, and cut the insert hole to shape with a jigsaw or scrollsaw. File the sides of the hole straight if necessary.

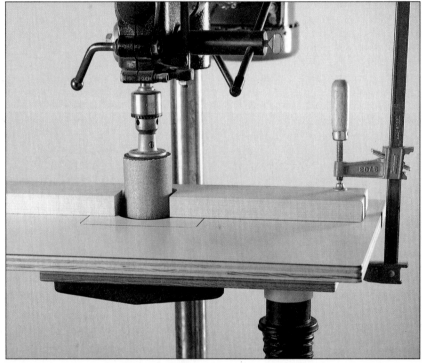

When you want to edge-sand with precision, start by bolting the table to the drill press. Then clamp the fence into position where shown, and attach a vacuum hose to the adapter.

4. Cut the table inserts (B) to size. (We cut a separate insert with a hole to match each different-sized sanding drum.) Apply laminate to the top and bottom of each insert; rout any overlap flush with the edges of the inserts. Sand the corners and edges so that the inserts fit snugly inside the tabletop cutout.

5. In the center of each insert, cut a hole ½″ larger in diameter than the diameter of the sanding drums you plan to use.

continued

In this photo you can see how we removed the drum-sanding insert for a better view of the dust-collection slot beneath it. Various inserts, each with a different-sized hole, will accommodate a range of drum-sander sizes.

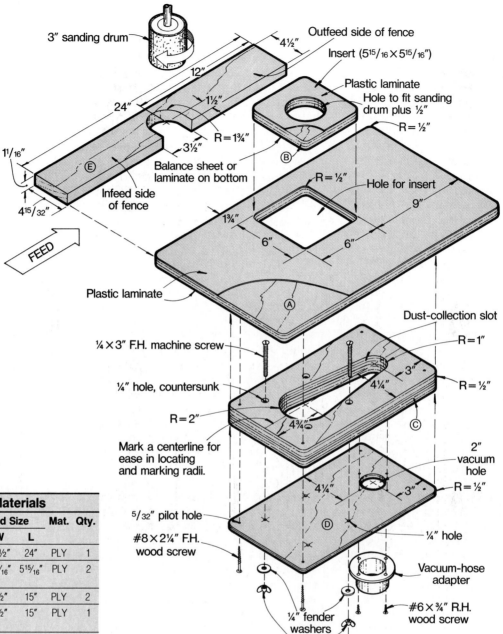

3″ sanding drum

Outfeed side of fence

Insert (5$^{15}/_{16}$ × 5$^{15}/_{16}$″)

Plastic laminate

Hole to fit sanding drum plus ½″

R = ½″

12″

4½″

24″

1½″

R = 1¾″

Balance sheet or laminate on bottom

Ⓑ

R = ½″

Hole for insert

9″

1$^1/_{16}$″

3½″

Ⓔ

1¾″

6″

6″

Infeed side of fence

4$^{15}/_{32}$″

FEED

Plastic laminate

Ⓐ

Dust-collection slot

R = 1″

¼ × 3″ F.H. machine screw

3″

4¼″

R = ½″

¼″ hole, countersunk

R = 2″

4¾″

Ⓒ

2″ vacuum hole

Mark a centerline for ease in locating and marking radii.

4¼″

3″

R = ½″

$^5/_{32}$″ pilot hole

Ⓓ

¼″ hole

#8 × 2¼″ F.H. wood screw

Vacuum-hose adapter

#6 × ¾″ R.H. wood screw

¼″ fender washers

¼″ wing nuts

Bill of Materials

Part	Finished Size			Mat.	Qty.
	T	W	L		
A tabletop	¾″	14½″	24″	PLY	1
B table insert	¾″	5$^{15}/_{16}$″	5$^{15}/_{16}$″	PLY	2
C subtable	¾″	8½″	15″	PLY	2
D bottom panel	¼″	8½″	15″	PLY	1
E sanding fence	1$^1/_{16}$″	4½″	24″	M	1

Material Key: PLY—plywood, M—maple.
Supplies: #6 × ¾″ roundhead wood screws, #8 × 2¼″ flathead wood screws, 4—¼ × 3″ flathead machine screws with fender washers and wing nuts (fender washers are wider than regular washers), plastic laminate, contact cement, polyurethane.

BOTTOM VIEW

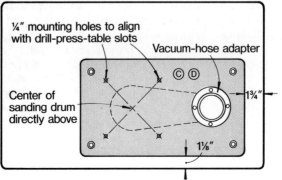

¼″ mounting holes to align with drill-press-table slots

Vacuum-hose adapter

Ⓒ Ⓓ

1¾″

Center of sanding drum directly above

1⅛″

65

DRUM-SANDING TABLE
continued

Make and attach the subtable assembly

1. Cut two pieces of ¾″ plywood to size for the subtable (C). Glue and clamp the pieces together with the edges flush. When the glue dries, cut the corners to shape, and sand the edges smooth.

2. Mark a centerline down the length of the subtable where shown on the Exploded View Drawing, page 65. Use the centerline and other dimensions given to lay out the shape of the dust-collection slot. Then drill a ⅜″ hole through the subtable to start the blade, and cut the slot to shape with a jigsaw.

3. Cut the bottom panel (D) to size from ¼″ plywood. Mark the location of the 2″ vacuum hole, and cut it out with a circle cutter, or cut it to shape with a jigsaw.

4. With the tabletop facedown, position the subtable and the bottom panel over the hole for the inserts, and dry-clamp them in place. Drill and countersink a ⁵⁄₃₂″ pilot hole in each corner of the assembly, drilling completely through the subtable and bottom panel, and ¼″ into the tabletop. Fasten the pieces together with four #8 × 2¼″ wood screws (do not use glue, because you need to be able to remove the tabletop from the subtable for ease of access when drilling the mounting-screw holes later).

Mount the table to your drill press

Note: Mounting-hole locations vary from one drill press to another. Try to position the holes inside the square cutout for easier access to the mounting screws.

1. Center your drill-press table under the drill-press spindle.

2. Set the sanding-table assembly on your drill-press table. Chuck a sanding drum in the drill press, and align the sanding table to center the sanding drum in the insert hole.

3. Securely clamp the sanding table to your drill-press table, and mark the location of the slots in the drill-press table to the bottom of part D.

4. Remove the sanding table from the drill press. Remove the screws and separate the tabletop from the subtable and bottom panel assembly. With the subtable and bottom panel still screwed together, use a drill press and a ¼″ bit to drill four mounting-bolt holes where marked on the bottom of the panel. Flip the assembly faceup and countersink the ¼″ holes. Insert a ¼ × 3″ machine screw in each hole, and reassemble the entire sanding-table assembly.

5. Position the sanding table over the drill-press table. Fasten the sanding table to the drill-press table with machine screws, washers, and wing nuts.

Make the fence and finish the assembly

1. From 1¹⁄₁₆″-thick maple, cut the sanding fence (E) to 4½ × 24″. Mark and cut the sanding-drum hole where dimensioned on the Exploded View Drawing. Using a tablesaw, rip the infeed side to 4¹⁵⁄₃₂″ (For safety's sake, rip only as far as the drum-sander hole, then turn the saw off, rather than trying to back the piece out with the saw running.)

2. Apply polyurethane to the exposed wood surfaces, and attach the vacuum-hose adapter to the table.

Using the drum-sanding table for edge-sanding

Fasten the drum-sanding table to your drill-press table with the machine screws, washers, and wing nuts. Then chuck a 3 × 3″ sanding drum in the drill-press chuck. Use a straightedge to align the edge of the sanding drum with the *outfeed* side of the fence. Once the fence is in position, clamp it to the drum-sanding table. Attach the vacuum hose to the vacuum-hose adapter, and start the vacuum and drill press. Feed the stock along the *infeed* side of the fence in the direction noted on the Exploded View Drawing. The stock will come in contact with the sanding drum and have ¹⁄₃₂″ sanded off when it reaches the outfeed side of the sanding fence.

Buying Guide
- **Two vacuum-hose adapters.** Part no. 516262, from Shopsmith, 3931 Image Dr., Dayton, OH 45414. Call 800-543-7586 or 513/898-6070 for price.
- **3″ sanding drum.** 3 × 3″, ⅜″ shank. For current price of drum and abrasive sleeves, contact Puckett Electric Tools, 841 Eleventh St., Des Moines, IA 50309, or call 800-544-4189 or 515/244-4189.

THICKNESS SANDER

Make your own thin stock by resawing thicker boards, then using this thickness sander to remove the saw marks. The sander also excels at truing up surfaces for cutting boards and other edge-joined projects.

The sturdy maple stand will take years of hard use, and the hood keeps the whole operation practically dust-free. The sander adjusts easily and can handle stock up to 2" thick and 12" wide.

Note: While several parts of the base are the same size (A and B, for example; see the Cutting Diagram on page 69), we call them out separately because they are mirror images of each other and need to be machined individually. To avoid making errors, we found it much easier to lay out the location of the joints before cutting.

Build the base

1. Rip and crosscut the feet (A, B), legs (C, D, E, F), top braces (G), and rails (H, I) to size.

2. Using the Parts View Drawing, page 70, and the Exploded View Drawing, page 68, lay out and mark the dadoes, rabbets, notches, and half-lap joints on pieces A, B, C, D, E, F, G, and H. (Since B is the mirror image of A, clamp A to B and mark both pieces at the same time for uniformity. Mark C and E, and D and F the same way.)

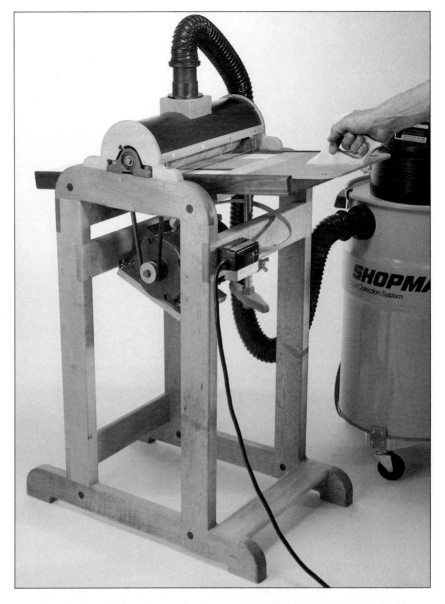

3. Using a saw fitted with a dado blade, cut the joints as marked. Make all identical cuts at the same time to ensure accuracy and to avoid having to reset the saw unnecessarily.

4. Glue and clamp the right-hand assembly (A–C–D–G) together where shown on the Exploded View Drawing. After the glue dries, locate and mark the center of each half-lap joint, then drill a ¾" hole through each, backing the workpiece with scrap

to prevent chip-out. Apply glue and insert a ¾" walnut dowel 1¾" long into each hole. Repeat this with the left-hand assembly (B–E–F–G), and sand the dowels flush after the glue dries.

5. Mark and cut a 2" radius on the top ends of A and B, and a 3" radius on the top corners of both leg assemblies. Cut the ¼" relief on the bottoms of A and B.

continued

THICKNESS SANDER
continued

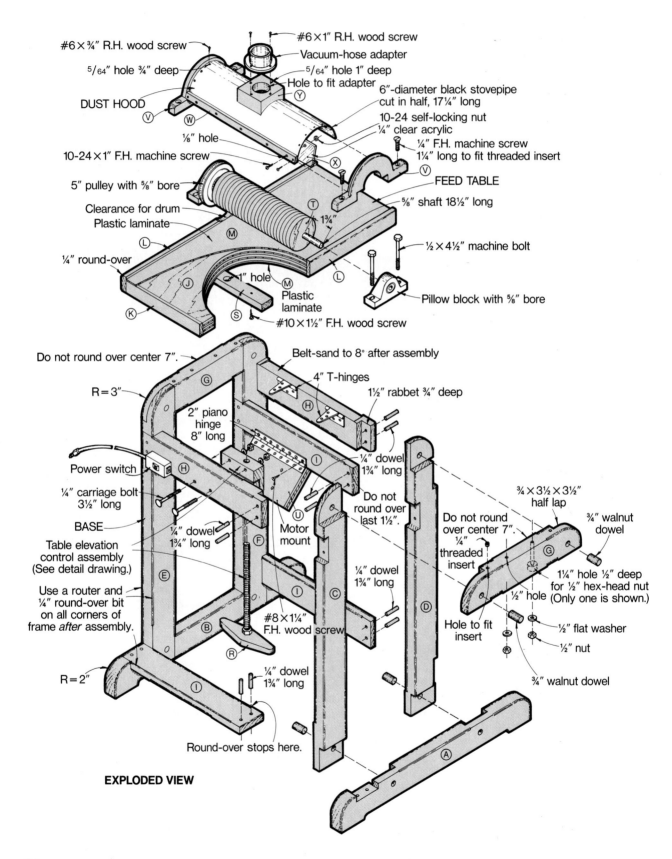

#6 × ¾" R.H. wood screw

#6 × 1" R.H. wood screw

⁵/₆₄" hole ¾" deep

Vacuum-hose adapter

⁵/₆₄" hole 1" deep

DUST HOOD

Hole to fit adapter

6"-diameter black stovepipe cut in half, 17¼" long

10-24 self-locking nut

¼" clear acrylic

⅛" hole

10-24 × 1" F.H. machine screw

¼" F.H. machine screw 1¼" long to fit threaded insert

5" pulley with ⅝" bore

FEED TABLE

⅝" shaft 18½" long

Clearance for drum

Plastic laminate

¼" round-over

1¾"

½ × 4½" machine bolt

1" hole

Plastic laminate

#10 × 1½" F.H. wood screw

Pillow block with ⅝" bore

Do not round over center 7".

Belt-sand to 8° after assembly

R = 3"

4" T-hinges

1½" rabbet ¾" deep

2" piano hinge 8" long

¾ × 3½ × 3½" half lap

Power switch

¼" dowel 1¾" long

¾" walnut dowel

¼" carriage bolt 3½" long

Do not round over center 7".

BASE

Do not round over last 1½".

¼" threaded insert

Table elevation control assembly (See detail drawing.)

Motor mount

¼" dowel 1¾" long

½" hole

1¼" hole ½" deep for ½" hex-head nut (Only one is shown.)

Use a router and ¼" round-over bit on all corners of frame *after* assembly.

¼" dowel 1¾" long

Hole to fit insert

½" flat washer

½" nut

#8 × 1¼" F.H. wood screw

¾" walnut dowel

R = 2"

¼" dowel 1¾" long

Round-over stops here.

EXPLODED VIEW

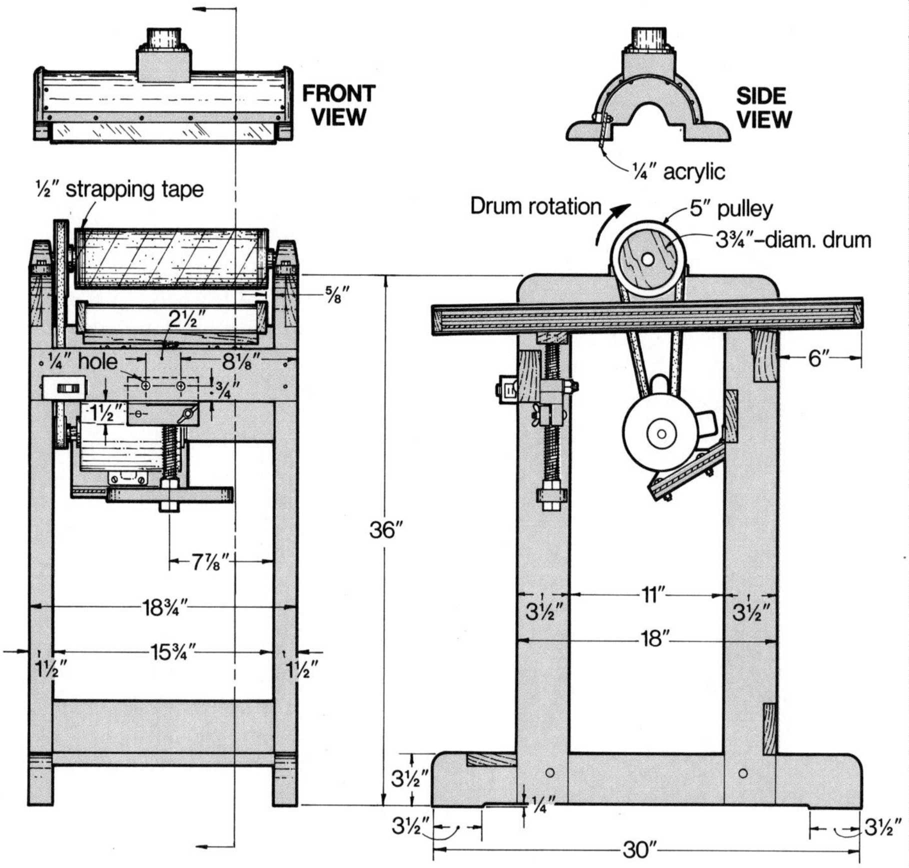

FRONT VIEW
SIDE VIEW
¼" acrylic
½" strapping tape
Drum rotation
5" pulley
3¾"-diam. drum
⅝"
2½"
¼" hole
8⅛"
¾"
1½"
6"
36"
7⅞"
18¾"
15¾"
1½"
1½"
11"
3½"
3½"
18"
3½"
¼"
3½"
3½"
30"

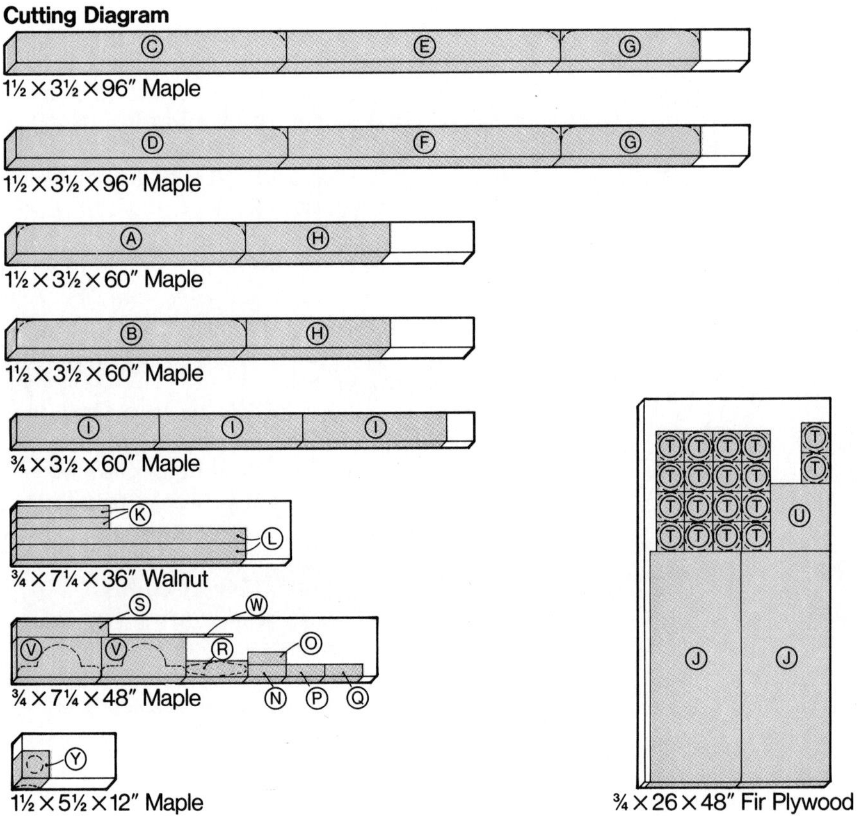

Cutting Diagram
C
E
G
1½ × 3½ × 96" Maple
D
F
G
1½ × 3½ × 96" Maple
A
H
1½ × 3½ × 60" Maple
B
H
1½ × 3½ × 60" Maple
I
I
I
¾ × 3½ × 60" Maple
K
L
¾ × 7¼ × 36" Walnut
S
W
V
V
R
O
N
P
Q
¾ × 7¼ × 48" Maple
Y
1½ × 5½ × 12" Maple
T
U
J
J
¾ × 26 × 48" Fir Plywood

Bill of Materials

Part	Finished Size* T	W	L	Mat.	Qty.
Base					
A foot	1½"	3½"	30"	M	1
B foot	1½"	3½"	30"	M	1
C leg	1½"	3½"	35¾"	M	1
D leg	1½"	3½"	35¾"	M	1
E leg	1½"	3½"	35¾"	M	1
F leg	1½"	3½"	35¾"	M	1
G brace	1½"	3½"	18"	M	2
H rail	1½"	3½"	18¾"	M	2
I rail	¾"	3½"	18¾"	M	3
Feed Table					
J* table	¾"	12⅛"	29"	PLY	2
K trim	½"	1½"	12⅛"	W	2
L trim	½"	1⅞"	30"	W	2
M* laminate	$\frac{1}{16}$"	12⅛"	30"	PL	2
Elevation Control					
N control	¾"	1½"	5"	M	1
O control	¾"	1½"	5"	M	1
P control	¾"	1½"	5"	M	1
Q control	¾"	1½"	5"	M	1
R handle	¾"	2"	8"	M	1
S holder	¾"	2"	12"	M	1
Remaining Parts					
T disc	¾"	3¾" diam.		PLY	18
U mount block	¾"	8½"	8"	PLY	1
V hood end	¾"	5"	11"	M	2
W strip	⅜"	¾"	17¼"	M	1
X strip	¼"	2¼"	15"	A	1
Y block	1½"	3½"	3½"	M	1
Z pushblock	¼"	12"	12"	HB	1
AA handle	¾"	5"	7"	M	1

*Parts marked with an * are cut larger initially, then trimmed to finished size. Please read the instructions before cutting.

Material Key: M—maple, PLY—plywood or particleboard, W—walnut, PL—plastic laminate, A—acrylic, HB—hardboard.

Supplies: ¾" walnut dowel, ¼" birch dowel, ¾" threaded rod 12" long w/3—¾" nuts, 4—¼ × 1¼" F.H. mach. screws and 4—¼" threaded inserts, ¼ × 3½" carr. bolts w/¼" washers and nuts, ⅜ × 2" carr. bolt w/wing nut and washer, #8 × 1¼" F.H. wood screw, #10 × 1½" F.H. wood screws, 4—½ × 4¼" mach. bolts w/washers and nuts, #6 × ¾" R.H. wood screws, #6 × 1" R.H. wood screws, 10-24 × 1" F.H. machine screws w/self-locking nuts, 2—4" steel T-hinges w/mounting screws, ¾-hp. (1,725-rpm) motor, 2" pulley to fit motor shaft, 5" pulley w/⅝" bore, ½ × 33" V-belt, 2 × 8" continuous hinge w/mounting screws, ⅝" steel rod 18½" long, 6" diam. stovepipe 17¼" long, epoxy, woodworker's glue, contact cement, strapping tape. See Buying Guide, page 73, for additional supplies.

THICKNESS SANDER
continued

PARTS VIEW

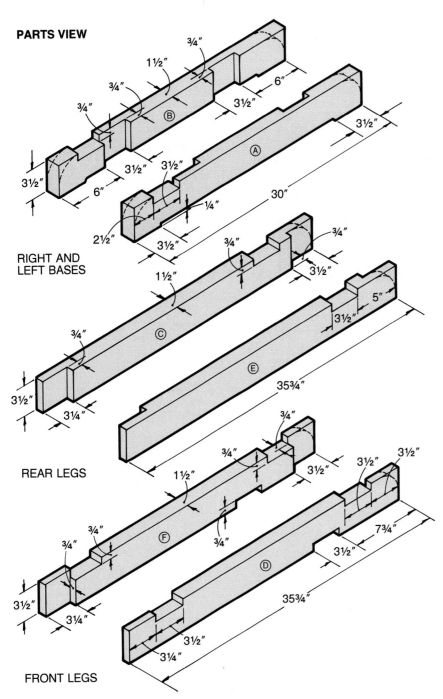

RIGHT AND
LEFT BASES

REAR LEGS

FRONT LEGS

6. Clamp H and I in position to join the leg assemblies. Mark the edges of H and I that will be enclosed in the joints. Disassemble and use a router fitted with a ¼" round-over bit to round over all edges of the leg assemblies *except* at the joint locations and on the top and bottom of both Gs where the pillow blocks will be mounted.

7. Glue and clamp H and I to the leg assemblies. After the glue dries, remove the clamps and drill two ¼" holes in each joint. Then glue and insert the dowels, sanding flush after the glue dries.

8. Belt-sand an 8° bevel the length of the back rail (H) to provide clearance when adjusting the feed table.

9. Sand the rounded corners and all surfaces smooth, and apply the finish.

Build the feed table
1. Cut two like-sized pieces of ¾" plywood (J) to size plus ½" in each direction. Laminate the two together, and after the glue dries, trim the lamination to its finished size (12⅛ × 29").

2. Rip and crosscut the walnut trim strips (K, L). Cut a clearance recess for the drum sander in the top center of each L. Glue and clamp one K to each end of the plywood lamination, with the top and ends flush with the ends of the plywood.

3. Cut the plastic laminate (M) slightly oversize and apply the laminate with contact cement. Then, using a router with a flush trimmer, trim the laminate. Glue and clamp the side trim strips (L) to the feed-table assembly.

4. Using a ¼" round-over bit, rout the outside edges of both Ls.

5. Attach the T-hinges to the bottom of the feed table. Then fasten the feed table to the back rail (H) ⅝" from the right leg assembly as dimensioned in the Front View Drawing, page 69.

Construct the elevation control

1. Cut the elevation control parts N, O, P, and Q to size as dimensioned in the Bill of Materials, page 69. Clamp N and O together, then clamp P to the top of N–O.

2. Drill and countersink holes for the two #10×1¼" screws through the top of P and ½" into N and O as shown in the Elevation Control Drawing, *below.* Screw P to N–O.

3. Clamp Q to the top of P, then drill and countersink holes for two #10×1¼" screws through the top of Q and ½" in P, and one through the side of N ½" into

O. Install the screws. Mark the location and drill a ⅜" hole through N–O for the ⅜" carriage bolt.

4. Drill a ¾" hole vertically through the entire assembly (N–O–P–Q) where indicated in the drawing for the ¾" threaded rod. Remove all the screws and drill a 1⅛" hole ⁷⁄₁₆" deep into the top of P and ³⁄₁₆" deep into the bottom of Q.

5. Disassemble the pieces, then thread a ¾" nut on the ¾" rod, and insert the rod through P. Trace the outline of the nut and chisel out the excess. Repeat this with Q. The recesses house the nut snugly, stopping it from turning with the rod.

6. With a fine-toothed saw, cut the rabbet and slot in the top and back side of N as shown in the Front and Side views of the Elevation Control Drawing. The gaps will allow you to lock the threaded rod in position, preventing changes in the height of the feed table caused by sanding vibrations. Apply glue to the mating surfaces of N and O, and screw the pieces together.

7. Apply glue to the mating surface of N–O and P, install the screws through P and into N–O, and allow the glue to dry. Install the carriage bolt and attach the washer and wing nut. *continued*

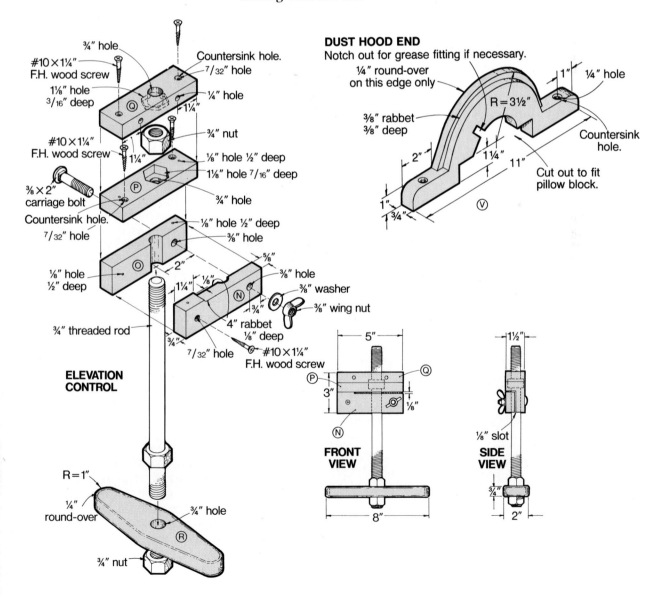

THICKNESS SANDER
continued

8. Insert the 12″ threaded rod through N–O, and thread it through the nut in place in P. With the nut in place, glue and fasten Q to the N–O–P assembly.

9. Drill two ¼″ holes through Q where indicated for later mounting to the front rail (H).

10. Cut the handle (R) to size and shape. Round over the outside corners with a ¼″ bit, then drill a ¾″ hole through its center. Secure the handle on the threaded rod with a ¾″ nut above and below the handle. Tighten the nuts to hold the handle firmly in position at the bottom of the threaded rod.

11. Position the elevation-control assembly where shown on the Front View and Side View drawings, page 71, and clamp it in place. Using the two previously drilled ¼″ holes in Q as guides, drill like-sized holes through the front rail. Bolt the elevation control to the rail.

12. Cut the rod-tip holder (S) to size. Locate the center of S and drill a 1″ hole through it. Slip S over the rod and crank up the rod into contact with the feed table. Align S squarely with the bottom of the table, clamp it in place, drill pilot holes, and install two #10×1½″ screws where shown on the Exploded View Drawing, page 68.

Construct and mount the drum

1. Rip and crosscut eighteen 3¾″ squares from ¾″ plywood, mark diagonals to find the center, and drill a ⅝″ hole in the center of each. Drill a ⅝″ hole in a piece of scrap plywood 1½″ from one edge, and place a ⅝″ dowel 2″ long in the hole. Clamp the jig to the bed of your bandsaw with

the center of the dowel 1⅞″ from the blade. Fit the squares one at a time onto the jig, and cut the 18 discs (T) to 3¾″ diameter as shown in photo A, *below.*

A

2. Rough up the ⅝″ steel shaft with a file, then, starting 1¾″ from the right-hand end, epoxy the discs to each other and to the shaft. Once all the discs are on the rod, clamp them together with three bar clamps.

3. Slip the 5″ pulley onto the left end of the drum shaft, and insert the ends of the shaft into the pillow blocks. Set the shaft assembly in place on the stand.

4. Center the pillow blocks on G, clamp them in position, and mark the mounting-hole locations. Remove the clamps and the pillow block/drum assembly. Drill ½″ holes completely through both Gs, and drill a 1¼″ hole ½″ deep on the bottom of the ½″ hole to house the ¾″ nut. Bolt the pillow blocks to the stand. Center the sanding drum over the feed table. Tighten the pulley setscrew, stop-collar setscrews, and the nuts on the bottom of the machine bolts.

5. Cut the motor mount block (U) to size, and attach the hinge to it.

6. Attach the 2″ pulley to motor shaft. Clamp the motor to the mounting block, and position the drive belt to align the pulleys. Drill the ⅜″ motor-mounting holes, secure the motor mount to part I, and bolt the motor to U.

Make the dust hood

1. Cut the dust hood ends (V) to shape as dimensioned in the Dust Hood End Drawing, page 71 (the shape of the pillow block used will determine the inside shape). With a rabbeting bit, rout a ⅜″ rabbet ⅜″ deep around the semicircular inside top edges of V. Drill and countersink ¼″ holes where indicated for later mounting of V to the stand.

2. Cut a 17¼″ length of 6″-diameter stovepipe in half lengthwise. Drill pilot holes through the pipe and into each V where shown in the Exploded View Drawing, page 68. Attach the stovepipe to V with #6×¾″ screws. (If you like, use 6″ PVC pipe in place of the stovepipe.)

3. Cut the maple strip (W) and acrylic strip (X) to size. Attach them to the hood assembly with machine screws. The acrylic provides a clear view of the sanding, yet it prevents fingers from getting too close to the abrasive action.

4. Cut part Y to size, then cut a hole through it and the stovepipe hood to match the diameter of the vacuum-hose adapter. Using a bandsaw, cut Y to fit the shape of the hood. Screw the adapter to Y and screw Y to the hood from the inside of the hood with #6×1″ roundhead wood screws.

5. Position the hood over the pillow blocks, and mark the mounting holes for the threaded inserts on both Gs. Drill the holes on the marks, and install the four threaded inserts.

6. Sand all remaining wood surfaces and apply the finish of your choice. Connect the power supply switch to the front of the stand assembly.

Sand the drum to size

1. Run a hose from your vacuum to the vacuum-hose adapter on the dust hood. Using contact cement or spray-on adhesive, attach two sheets of 60-grit sandpaper to a piece of ¾″ plywood 13¾″ wide by 12″ long. Attach this to another piece of plywood or particleboard the same width as the feed table (12″). Raise the feed table until the sanding board just makes contact with the laminated drum. Plug the motor into the power-supply switch, then plug the cord running from the switch into an outlet. Turn on the sander and vacuum, and slowly feed the sanding board under the drum as shown in photo B, *below.*

Caution: Feed the sanding board through from the front side only. Continue to sand and raise the feed table with the elevation control until the sanding drum is uniformly round over its entire length. (This sanding ensures that the sanding drum is parallel with the feed table.)

2. See the Buying Guide for our source of Velcro mat and sandpaper strip. Instructions for adhering the mat to the sanding drum and the sandpaper to the mat are included with each order.

Note: Use 60- and 80-grit paper on the drum to remove unevenness remaining after resawing or for thickness sanding. For progressively smoother finishes, use 100-, 120-, and 150-grit paper.

Using the thickness sander

1. Raise the table so that the bottom of the drum just touches the top of the material to be sanded, then lock the elevation control.

2. Slowly and steadily feed the material from the front side only, pushing the material on through the sander using the pushblock as shown in the Pushblock Drawing, *below.*

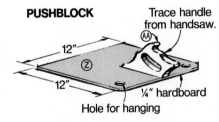

PUSHBLOCK

Trace handle from handsaw.

12″

12″

¼″ hardboard

Hole for hanging

3. Unlock the elevation control and raise the table by turning the handle *no more* than an eighth of a turn at a time. Relock the elevation control. Repeat step 2, and again raise an eighth of a turn and sand to the desired thickness or smoothness.

Buying Guide

- **Two vacuum-hose adapters.** Part no. 516262, from Shopsmith, 3931 Image Dr., Dayton, OH 45414. Call 800-543-7586 or 513/898-6070 for price.
- **Power switch.** Catalog no. A526. Contact AMT, P.O. Box 70, Royersford, PA 19468, or call 215/948-0400, for current price.
- **Ball-bearing pillow blocks.** Rigid-mount VPLE series, ⅝″ bore with stop collars. For the current price, contact Standard Bearings, 2350 Hubbell Ave., Des Moines, IA 50317, or call 800-554-8123 or 515/265-5261.
- **Velcro mat and sandpaper strip.** Velcro mat, 3×77″; catalog no. 18VMW. Felt-backed sandpaper, 3×77″; grits range from 40 to 220. Instructions for attaching the Velcro mat and sandpaper included. Contact Woodmaster Tools, 2908 Oak, Dept. WDS, Kansas City, MO 64108. Or call 800-821-6651 or 816/756-2195.

SHOP ORGANIZERS

Tired of groping for tools and jury-rigging ways to get a simple job done? This chapter offers 11 projects that can get your woodworking act together once and for all.

ONE-WEEKEND WORKBENCH

What more could a home woodworker want? The workbench, *opposite,* is inexpensive, sturdy, and you can tackle it in just one weekend. It's equipped with an ingenious shop-built end vise, a tool tray, and lots of other conveniences.

Build the base

Note: Refer to the Exploded View Drawing and Cutting Diagram on pages 76 and 77, as well as the End Section Drawing at right.

1. Rip ¼″ from each edge of all the 2×4 stock for a 3″ finished width. (This removes factory-rounded edges and lets you make tighter-fitting, better-looking joints.) Crosscut the legs (A), end rails (B), and cross members (C, D) to size. Cut the strut (E) to size plus 2″ in length, and cut the vise-bar guide (F) to size.

2. Measure and mark the half-lap joint locations on the ends of the legs and rails. Using a dado blade on a radial-arm saw or tablesaw, test-cut half-lap joints on two pieces of scrap of the same thickness as the dimensioned pine stock. Check the fit and adjust the depth of cut if necessary. Clamp a stop to the saw fence to ensure an equal 3″ half lap on all parts. Cut the joints on the ends of A and B.

3. At the same depth of cut used for the half-lap joints, cut a dado in the center of the bottom rails (B) for cross member D.

4. Glue and clamp the leg/rail assemblies (A, B) together, checking for square with a framing square.

5. Drill ¾″ holes centered on each of the bottom half-lap joints only. You will drill the top dowel holes later when joining the cross members to the leg/rail assemblies. (To prevent splintering, we drilled with a

spade bit until just the tip of the bit poked through the opposite side of the board. Then we turned the assembly over and, using the hole as a guide, finished drilling through the joint.)

6. Cut four ¾″ walnut dowels 1⅝″ long, and glue them into the holes in the bottom half-lap

joints. After the glue dries, belt-sand the dowels flush. Cut a 1½″ radius on the four bottom corners; sand them smooth.

7. Glue and clamp the cross members (C, D) between the leg/rail assemblies. Bore ¾″ dowel holes through the upper half-lap joints and 1½″ into the ends of the cross *continued*

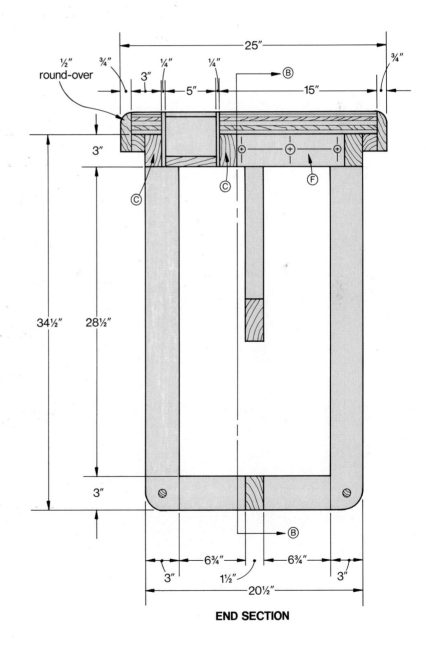

END SECTION

ONE-WEEKEND WORKBENCH
continued

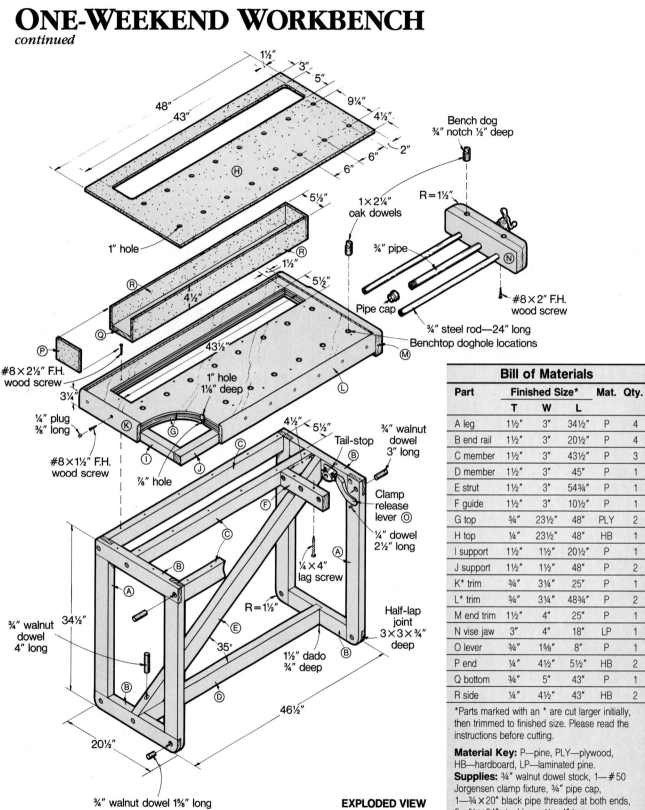

Bill of Materials				
Part	**Finished Size***			**Mat.**	**Qty.**
	T	**W**	**L**		
A leg	1½"	3"	34½"	P	4
B end rail	1½"	3"	20½"	P	4
C member	1½"	3"	43½"	P	3
D member	1½"	3"	45"	P	1
E strut	1½"	3"	54¾"	P	1
F guide	1½"	3"	10½"	P	1
G top	¾"	23½"	48"	PLY	2
H top	¼"	23½"	48"	HB	1
I support	1½"	1½"	20½"	P	1
J support	1½"	1½"	48"	P	2
K* trim	¾"	3¼"	25"	P	1
L* trim	¾"	3¼"	48¾"	P	2
M end trim	1½"	4"	25"	P	1
N vise jaw	3"	4"	18"	LP	1
O lever	¾"	1⅝"	8"	P	1
P end	¼"	4½"	5½"	HB	2
Q bottom	¾"	5"	43"	P	1
R side	¼"	4½"	43"	HB	2

*Parts marked with an * are cut larger initially, then trimmed to finished size. Please read the instructions before cutting.

Material Key: P—pine, PLY—plywood, HB—hardboard, LP—laminated pine.

Supplies: ¾" walnut dowel stock, 1—#50 Jorgensen clamp fixture, ¾" pipe cap, 1—¾×20" black pipe threaded at both ends, 2—¾×24" steel bars, ¼×4" lag screws, #8×1¼" F.H. wood screws, #8×1½" F.H. wood screws, #8×2" F.H. wood screws, #8×2½" F.H. wood screws, double-faced tape, 1" oak dowel stock, ¼" pine dowel stock, ½" brads, varnish, oil finish.

EXPLODED VIEW

members. Cut ¾″ walnut dowels
3″ long, then glue and insert the
dowels through the half-lap joints
and into the ends of the cross
members. After the glue dries,
remove the clamps and sand the
dowel ends flush.

8. Cut the angled ends of the
strut (E), then glue, clamp, and
dowel E into position. After the
glue dries, sand the entire base
assembly smooth.

Construct the workbench top

1. Rip the plywood pieces (G)
and hardboard (H) to size. (We
used double-faced tape to bond
the two pieces of plywood and
one piece of hardboard, then cut
all three pieces at one time for
uniformity.)

2. Glue and clamp the two
pieces of plywood together, being
careful to keep all four edges
flush. After the glue dries, mark
the location of the tool tray
where shown on the Exploded
View Drawing, *opposite.* Drill a
hole large enough for a jigsaw
blade and cut the opening to size.
(The tool tray fits snugly between
two cross members [C]).

3. Rip and crosscut support
pieces I and J to size. Glue and
clamp them to the bottom of the
plywood flush with the outside
edges. Remove any glue squeeze-
out from the outside edges.

4. Position the plywood top
(G) on the base assembly. Drill
pilot holes, then glue and screw
the top to the base using
#8×2½″ wood screws.

5. Rip and crosscut trim pieces
K and L to size plus 1″ in length.
Cut M to size then set it aside for
now. Miter-cut one end of each L
and both ends of K to finished
length.

continued

Cutting Diagram

6 pieces 2×4×96″ Pine

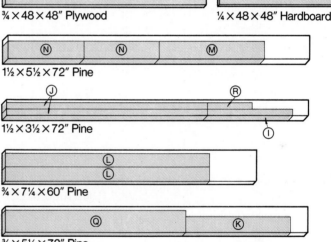

¾×48×48″ Plywood   ¼×48×48″ Hardboard

1½×5½×72″ Pine

1½×3½×72″ Pine

¾×7¼×60″ Pine

¾×5½×72″ Pine

ONE-WEEKEND WORKBENCH
continued

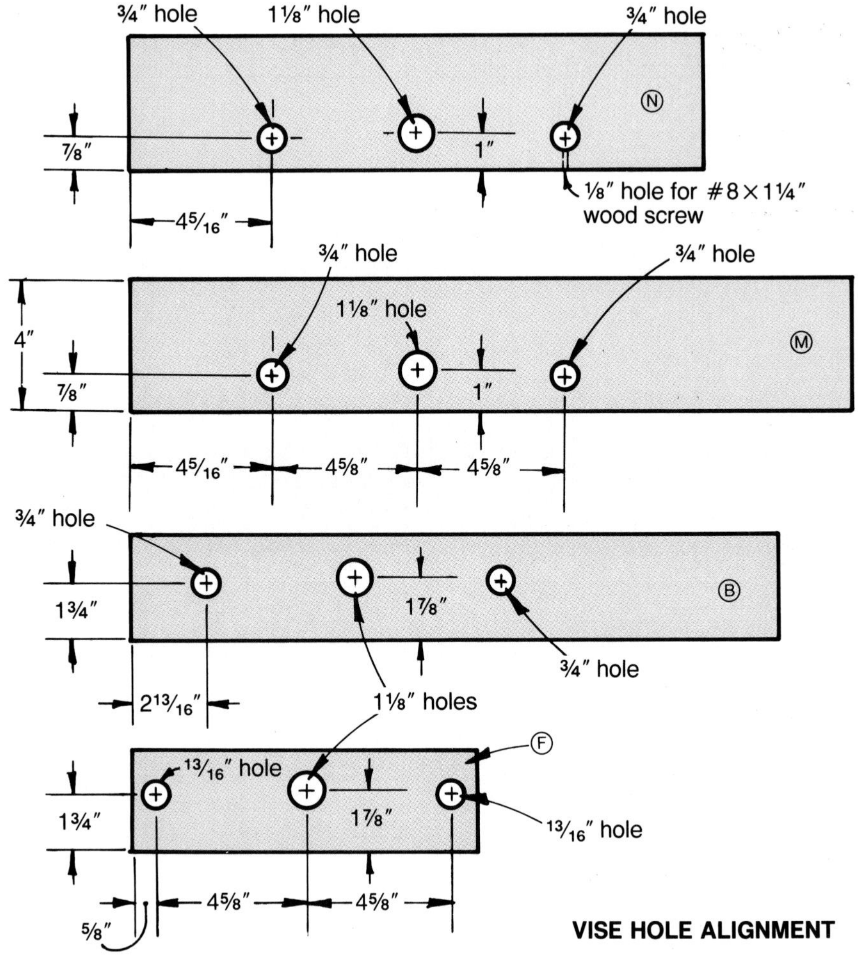

¾″ hole
1⅛″ hole
¾″ hole
Ⓝ
⅞″
1″
⅛″ hole for #8 × 1¼″ wood screw
4⁵⁄₁₆″
¾″ hole
¾″ hole
1⅛″ hole
Ⓜ
4″
⅞″
1″
4⁵⁄₁₆″
4⅝″
4⅝″
¾″ hole
Ⓑ
1¾″
1⅞″
¾″ hole
2¹³⁄₁₆″
1⅛″ holes
Ⓕ
¹³⁄₁₆″ hole
1¾″
1⅞″
¹³⁄₁₆″ hole
4⅝″
4⅝″
⅝″

VISE HOLE ALIGNMENT

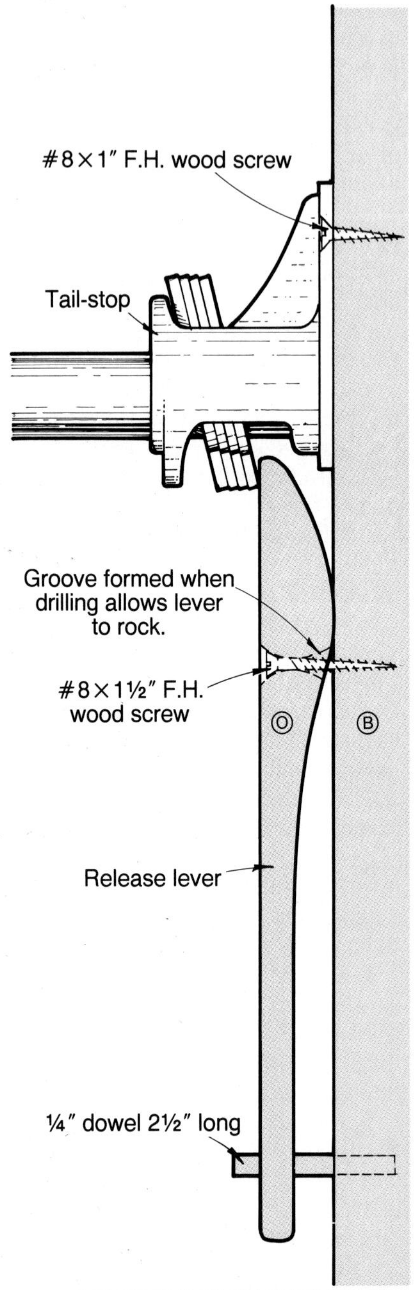

#8 × 1″ F.H. wood screw
Tail-stop
Groove formed when drilling allows lever to rock.
#8 × 1½″ F.H. wood screw
Ⓞ
Ⓑ
Release lever
¼″ dowel 2½″ long

QUICK RELEASE DETAIL

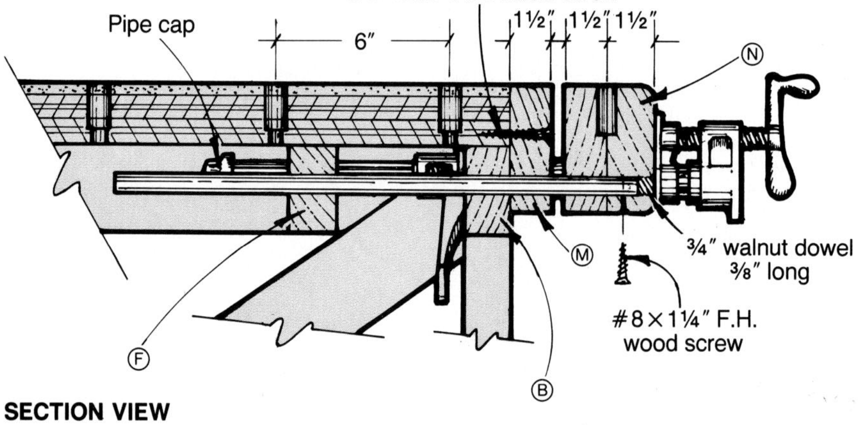

#8 × 2½″ F.H. wood screw
Pipe cap
6″
1½″
1½″
1½″
Ⓝ
¾″ walnut dowel ⅜″ long
Ⓜ
#8 × 1¼″ F.H. wood screw
Ⓕ
Ⓑ

SECTION VIEW

TOP VIEW   SIDE VIEW

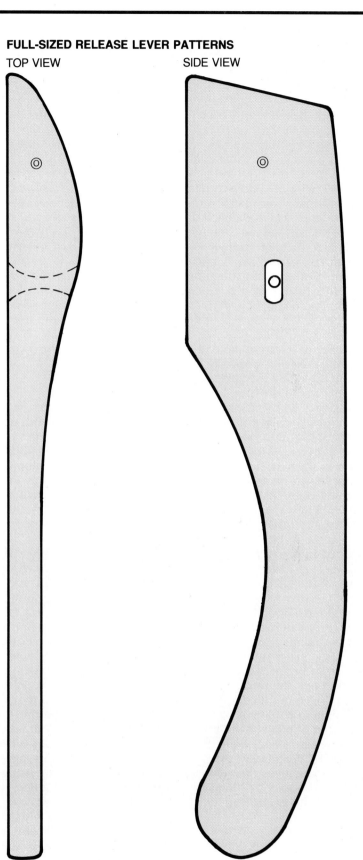

6. Position the hardboard (H) on top of the plywood. Drill ¼″ holes ⅜″ deep for plugs along the outside edges of pieces K and L. Drill a pilot hole through the center of each plug hole for the #8 × 1½″ wood screws used to attach the trim pieces to the benchtop. Glue and screw the trim pieces to the bench, flush with the top of the hardboard.

7. Cut ¼″ pine plugs ½″ long, then glue and insert them over the wood screws. Belt-sand the plugs flush with the trim pieces.

Build and install the vise

Note: This quick-clamp end vise, first featured separately in WOOD® *magazine, made a real hit with readers. It's a simple device that does the job of vises costing several times more.*

1. Laminate two pieces of ¾″-thick pine to form the vise jaw (N). Bore two ¾″ holes for the guide rods and one 1⅛″ hole for the black pipe through end-trim piece M as dimensioned on the Vise Hole Alignment Drawing, *opposite.*

2. Clamp M to N and, using the holes you already drilled in M as a positioning guide, drill like-sized holes through N. Glue and fasten M to the workbench top using #8 × 2″ wood screws covered with plugs. Drill corresponding holes through top rail B, again using M as a guide.

3. Cut two ¾″ steel rods to 24″ and one ¾″ black pipe (outside dimension 1¹⁄₁₆″) to 20″.

4. Cut two ¾″ walnut dowels ⅜″ long and glue them into the holes in the vise jaw (N) to cover the bar ends as shown in the Section View Drawing, *opposite.*
continued

ONE-WEEKEND WORKBENCH
continued

5. Bore holes in F as dimensioned in the Vise Hole Alignment Drawing, page 78. Position F under the workbench top and install the pipe and bars to align F with M. Drill two pilot holes through F and fasten it to the bottom of the workbench top with ¼ × 4″ lag screws.

6. Install the guide bars through vise parts N, M, B, and the pipe-clamp tail-stop, then on through F. Fasten the pipe-clamp tail-stop to rail B with a #8 × 1″ wood screw where shown in the Quick Release Detail, page 78. Attach the pipe cap to the end of the pipe under the workbench top and the crank mechanism to the other end of the pipe.

7. Using a ⅛″ metal-cutting bit, drill a hole 1¼″ deep through the bottom of N and through the center of each guide bar as shown in the Vise Hole Alignment and Section View drawings, page 78. Install #8 × 1¼″ screws to hold the guide bars in place.

8. Cut the lever O to size as indicated in the Full-Sized Release Lever Patterns, page 79, then drill the ⅛″ hole where indicated. Now wiggle the bit from side to side to form a groove so the lever can rock back and forth on the mounting screw (again, see patterns).

9. Fasten the release lever (O) so it rocks on the inside of top rail B. The end of the lever is positioned to release the spring-loaded tail-stop as shown in the Quick Release Detail. Now drill a ¼″ hole ¾″ deep below the handle of the lever, then glue and install a ¼″ dowel 2½″ long to keep the lever horizontal.

Note: To use the vise, pull the release lever toward top rail B. This releases the tail-stop, allowing you to pull the vise outward. When you reach the desired clamping distance, release the lever and give the clamp a quick jerk to set the tail-stop on the black pipe. Insert the project to be clamped and tighten the screw handle.

10. Clamp N tightly against M. Using a ½″ round-over bit, rout the top outside edge of the benchtop, being sure not to rout where M and N meet. Sand the round-over and pine pieces smooth.

Make the tool tray

1. Rip and crosscut the tool-tray pieces (P, Q, R) to size. Glue and nail the hardboard sides (R) to the pine bottom (Q), then nail the ends (P) to the pine bottom.

2. Insert the tool tray into the hole cut in the plywood top, and nail through the sides and ends to attach it to the benchtop.

Assemble the workbench

1. Apply double-faced tape to the plywood top (G), and set the hardboard in place, noting the location of the tool-tray cavity. (Carpet tape worked fine for us, but you may want to flush-mount a few screws to hold down the hardboard.) Don't glue it in position—you may want to replace the board in the future. Drill a hole through the hardboard and into the cavity large enough for a flush-cutting router bit. Fit your router with a flush-cutting bit and, using the tool-tray sides as a guide, rout the hardboard opening to size.

2. Bore 1″ bench dogholes 1¼″ deep through the benchtop (G, H) as spaced in the Exploded

View Drawing, page 76. Bore corresponding holes in vise part N. Center-bore a ⅞″ hole through the rest of the plywood bottom (G) to allow sawdust to fall through the doghole. Cut 1″ oak dowels 2¼″ long for the bench dogholes, then cut a ¾″ notch ½″ deep in one end of each. (We clamped each dowel in our newly constructed bench vise, and cut the notch with a handsaw.)

3. Finish-sand the entire assembly, then oil or varnish the pine, and oil the hardboard top.

Woodworker's Vise

The vise shown *below* is a smaller version of the end vise we made for the One-Weekend Workbench. This one mounts on the front of workbenches. We followed the same construction process, but added box-jointed walnut ends to the maple. We cut the box joints on the tablesaw. This smaller version uses ½″ pipe rather than ¾″ and a Jorgensen #52 rather than #50 clamp fixture.

PLANE RACK

S toring planes on a rack like this one not only keeps them conveniently together, it also safeguards the blades against nicks. And, it makes a handsome display as well.

Note: The final size of your rack and the position of each plane on it will depend on the size and number of planes you have. Use the photo and drawings of our rack as guides to help you build one to suit your needs.

1. Cut the backboard (A), trim pieces (B, C), positioners (D), rotating hold-downs (E), and lift pads (F) to size. Cut the heel plates to fit your planes (we formed ours to keep the plane heel from sliding left or right).

2. Cut the supports for the router plane and cutters if needed.

3. Position your planes on the backboard and mark the location of the positioners, rotating hold-downs, and heel plates.

4. Drill pilot holes and screw the heel plates to the backboard. Glue the lift pads in position; glue and nail the positioners in place.

5. Paint the backboard assembly and apply a clear finish to the trim and hold-downs. Screw the hold-downs in position, leaving the screws a bit loose so the hold-downs will rotate. Attach the trim.

6. Drill the holes through the plywood backboard, then fasten the rack to the wall.

Bill of Materials

Part	Finished Size			Mat.	Qty.
	T	W	L		
A backboard	¾"	17½"	29½"	PLY	1
B trim	¼"	¾"	30"	P	2
C trim	¼"	¾"	17½"	P	2
D positioner	⅜"	⅜"	2"	P	10
E hold-down	¾"	1¾"	1¾"	P	3
F lift pad	¼"	¾"	2"	P	5

Material Key: PLY—plywood, P—pine.
Supplies: #8 × 1¼" roundhead wood screws, #8 × 1½" flathead wood screws, 4d finish nails, paint, clear finish.

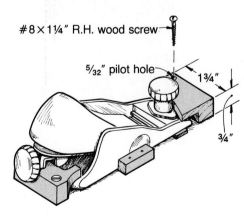

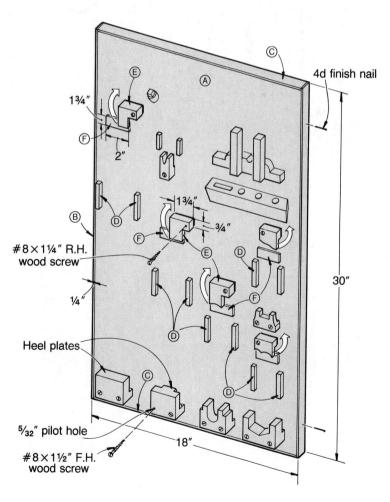

MODULAR WORKBENCH GROUP

Organize your tools and your work space with our interchangeable workbench group.

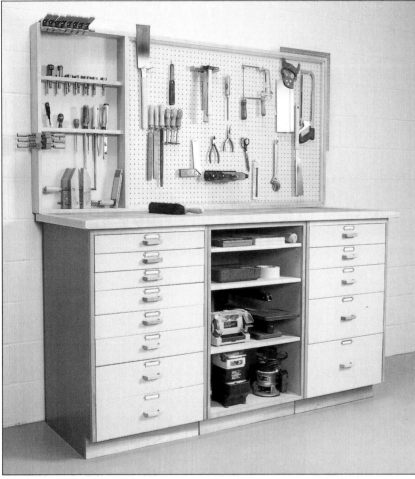

Basic cabinet and rack (opposite)

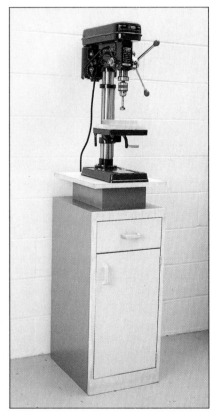

Drill-press stand (page 89)

Multi-tool storage unit (page 86)

Drawer bridge/cabinet (page 88)

Scrap bin/storage unit (page 87)

Basic Cabinet and Rack

All workshops vary considerably, and the component system shown opposite *takes this fact into account. You can select a grouping from the options shown, or even use some of the ideas we present and come up with a system of your own. We've designed lots of goodies into these units, so here's hoping you like what you see.*

Construct the cabinet carcass

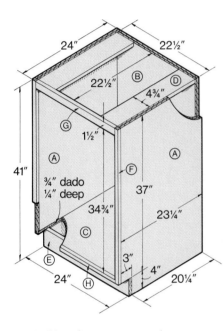

1. Rip, then crosscut the cabinet sides (A), back (B), bottom (C), cleats (D), and toekick (E) to size. (We laid out pieces A, B, and C on a sheet of plywood, then two of us cut them on a tablesaw. The job required four hands because one of us guided the piece through the saw while the other supported the panel.)

2. Cut a ¾" dado ¼" deep 4" from the bottom edge of the sides to receive the bottom (C). Cut a notch in the front lower corner of the sides. (This notched-out area creates the cabinet's toekick.)

Bill of Materials

Part	Finished Size*			Mat.	Qty.
	T	W	L		
Basic Cabinet Carcass					
A side	¾"	23¼"	41"	PLY	2
B back	¾"	22½"	41"	PLY	1
C bottom	¾"	22½"	23"	PLY	1
D cleat	¾"	4¾"	22½"	P	2
E toekick	¾"	4"	24"	P	1
F face frame	¾"	¾"	37"	P	2
G face frame	¾"	1½"	22½"	P	1
H face frame	¾"	¾"	22½"	P	1
For a 3⅛"-High Drawer					
I front	¾"	3⅛"	22⅜"	P	1
J side	½"	3"	22½"	P	2
K back	½"	2⅜"	21"	P	1
L bottom	¼"	21"	22⅜"	HB	1
Drawer Organizer					
M front/back	⅛"	1¾"	4"	HB	2
N side	½"	1¾"	3"	P	2
O bottom	⅛"	4"	4"	HB	1
Shelf					
P shelf	¾"	22¼"	22⅛"	PLY	1
Q trim	¾"	¾"	22⅛"	P	1
Benchtop					
R top	¾"	24½"	72½"	PLY	1
S top	¼"	24½"	72½"	HB	1
T* trim	1½"	1½"	75½"	P	1
U* trim	1½"	1½"	26"	P	2
Tool Rack					
V rail	¾"	3½"	73½"	P	2
W stile	¾"	3½"	36"	P	2
X divider	¾"	3½"	34½"	P	1
Y holder	¾"	3"	18⅝"	P	2
Z backing	¼"	18¾"	35¼"	HB	1
AA tool board	¼"	34½"	54¾"	PHB	1
BB frame	¾"	2½"	54¾"	P	2
CC frame	¾"	2½"	33"	P	3
DD molding	¾"	¾"	34½"	QR	2
EE molding	¾"	¾"	54¾"	QR	2

*Parts marked with an * are cut larger initially, then trimmed to finished size. Please read instructions carefully before cutting.

Material Key: PLY—plywood, P—pine, HB—hardboard, PHB—perforated hardboard, QR—quarter round.

Supplies: drawer pulls, 22" drawer slides, 18—#6x¾" flathead wood screws, shelf support clips, paint, polyurethane.

3. Glue, clamp, and nail the cabinet carcass together where shown on the cabinet-carcass drawing at *far left.* While the glue is still wet, check for square with a framing square. (You may have to rack it into square with pipe clamps.)

4. Cut the face-frame pieces (F, G, H) to size. Then glue, clamp, and nail them to the front of the cabinet carcass.

5. Sand all surfaces smooth. Mask the face frame and toekick, then paint the carcass. Later, finish the pine parts with oil.

Assemble the drawers

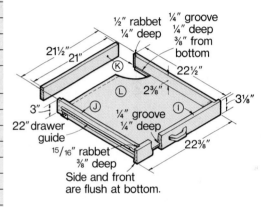

Note: In the Bill of Materials, we specify dimensions for a 3⅛"-high drawer. See the Assembled Cabinet Drawing, page 85, for the heights of the other drawers.

1. To make the drawers, rip, then crosscut the drawer fronts (I), sides (J), back (K), and bottom (L) to size.

2. Cut a ¼" groove ¼" deep and ⅜" up from the bottom of the fronts and sides where shown on the drawer drawing, *above.* Cut ¹⁵⁄₁₆" rabbets ⅜" deep on the ends of the drawer front.

3. Glue, clamp, and nail the drawers together. Nail the bottom (L) to the bottom edge of the back (K), but do not glue the drawer bottom into the groove; it should float in the joint. Remove glue squeeze-out before it dries. After the glue has dried, sand the drawers smooth. *continued*

MODULAR WORKBENCH GROUP
continued

4. Install drawer-slide hardware to the sides of the carcass and to the drawer sides. Paint the drawer fronts, then attach pulls to them.

Build the drawer organizers

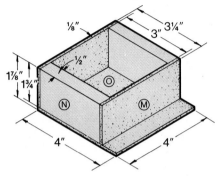

Note: Five drawer organizers per row fit nicely side by side. We've specified the dimensions for one organizer in the Bill of Materials, page 83. (To keep the organizers in good order, we nailed a cleat behind the back row.)

1. Cut the front and back (M), sides (N), and bottom (O) to size. Then glue and clamp the parts together as shown in the drawing *above.*

2. Sand all surfaces smooth, then paint.

Build a shelf

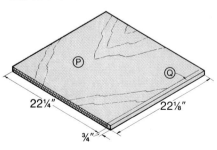

1. Cut the plywood (P) and the pine trim (Q) to size. Glue and nail the pine trim to the front edge of the plywood (see the drawing *above*).

2. Sand the pieces flush, mask the pine, then paint the plywood. After the paint has dried, remove the masking tape and apply oil finish to the pine.

3. Drill ¼" holes ½" deep on the inside of the cabinet sides (1½" in from the front and back) to house the shelf supports.

Make the benchtop

1. Cut the plywood (R) and the hardboard (S) to size. Position the hardboard above the plywood, flush on all edges. Then drive and countersink screws to hold the hardboard to the plywood. By fastening the two together in this way, you'll be

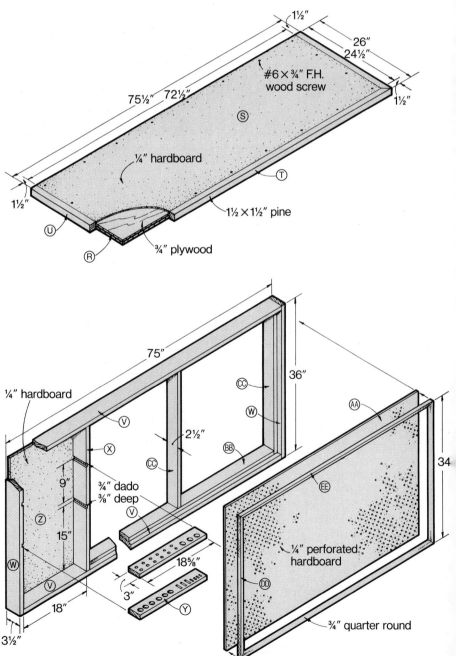

able to flip the hardboard over or replace it with a new piece when it gets battered. Sand all four edges smooth.

2. Cut the pine trim pieces (T, U) to length plus 1″ to allow for trimming. Miter-cut both ends of the front trim piece (T) and one end each of the two end trim pieces (U).

3. Test the fit against R–S and trim if necessary. Nail the trim pieces flush with the top of the hardboard as shown in the benchtop drawing, *opposite,* leaving a ½″ lip on the bottom.

4. Sand all surfaces smooth. Apply the finish to the top and trim. (This size benchtop fits nicely over three cabinets.)

Construct the tool rack

1. To make the basic framework, cut the top and bottom rails (V), stiles (W), center divider (X), and tool holders (Y) to size. Drill holes in the holders to fit your tools. Cut ¾″ dadoes ⅜″ deep in the left-hand stile (W) and center divider (X) to accept the racks.

2. Glue, clamp, and nail the framework (V, W, X) together (see the tool-rack drawing, *opposite*), using a framing square to check for square. (We did not glue or nail the racks [Y] into place, just in case we would ever want to change the arrangement or size of the holes.)

3. Cut the hardboard backing (Z) and the perforated hardboard (AA) to size. Rout a ⅜″ rabbet ¼″ deep around the portion of the frame the hardboard fits into, then chisel the corners square. Check the fit of both the perforated hardboard and the hardboard in their respective openings. Trim, if necessary, then paint both backing pieces. After the paint has dried, glue and nail the hardboard (Z) in place.

4. Cut parts BB and CC to size (these fit behind and support the perforated hardboard). Glue and nail them in place flush with the back edge of the main frame (V, W, X).

5. Lay a bead of glue on the front edge of BB and CC, then set the perforated hardboard in from the front side.

6. Miter-cut the quarter-round pieces (DD, EE) to length, and nail around the perimeter of the perforated hardboard. Finish the pine pieces. *continued*

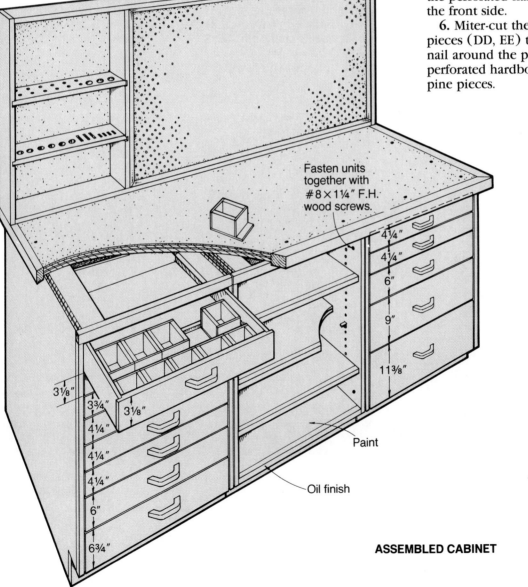

Fasten units together with #8 × 1¼″ F.H. wood screws.

4¼″
4¼″
6″
9″
11⅜″

3⅛″
3¾″
3⅛″
4¼″
4¼″
6″
6¾″

Paint

Oil finish

ASSEMBLED CABINET

MODULAR WORKBENCH GROUP
continued

Multi-Tool Storage Unit

Of all the modules we built, this one ranks No. 1 in variety. It boasts built-in blade storage and a slide-out tool caddy that houses often-used tools. Two drawers and adjustable shelves round out this hardworking module.

Build the cabinet carcass as described on page 83, except set back the bottom piece of the face frame ¾" to act as a stop. Cut to size and install the center divider (A), the horizontal support (B), and the shelves (C).

Cut the pieces for the pullout caddy (D, E, F, G, H, I, J). Then cut the grooves, rabbets, and dadoes, and assemble. Attach the caddy to the carcass with the 22" full-extension drawer slides. Rip and crosscut the drawer parts (K, L, M, N) to size. Assemble the two drawers as described on pages 83 and 84, using the dimensions listed in the Bill of Materials *left*. Cut the door (O) and blade holders (P, Q, R, S, T, U) to size, and assemble.

Mask the pine and paint the rest; remove the tape and finish the pine. Let dry and attach the hardware where shown *below*.

Multi-tool storage unit

Bill of Materials

Part	Finished Size			Mat.	Qty.
	T	**W**	**L**		
Carcass					
A divider	¾"	22½"	36¼"	PLY	1
B support	¾"	2"	13¾"	P	1
C shelf	½"	13½"	20½"	PLY	2
Pullout Caddy					
D front	¾"	7⅞"	34¾"	PLY	1
E side	½"	22"	33¾"	PLY	1
F back	½"	7"	33¾"	PLY	1
G rail	½"	4¼"	22"	PLY	1
H shelf	¾"	6½"	22⅛"	PLY	2
I rail	¼"	6½"	22⅛"	HB	1
J rail	½"	3"	22"	PLY	1
Drawer					
K front	¾"	3⁵⁄₁₆"	13⅝"	PLY	2
L back	½"	2¹³⁄₁₆"	12⅛"	PLY	2
M side	½"	3⁵⁄₁₆"	22⅝"	PLY	4
N bottom	¼"	12⅛"	22½"	HB	2
Door					
O door	¾"	13⁹⁄₁₆"	28"	PLY	1
P holder	¾"	1⅜"	8½"	P	1
Q holder	¾"	1⅜"	7"	P	2
R holder	⅛"	4"	10"	HB	1
S holder	⅛"	6½"	12¾"	HB	1
T holder	¾"	1¾"	11¼"	P	1
U holder	¾"	1¾"	9⅝"	P	2

Material Key: PLY—plywood, P—pine, HB—hardboard.
Supplies: paint, 2 pairs—22" drawer slides, 4—wood pulls, 2—2" F.H. wood screws, polyurethane finish, 2—cabinet locks, 2 pairs—22" full-extension drawer slides, 4—#8 × 1¾" F.H. wood screws, 8—shelf support clips.

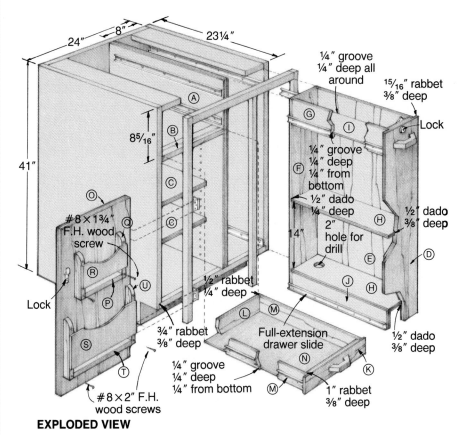

EXPLODED VIEW

Scrap Bin/Storage Drawer Unit

If you're like us, you find it oh, so hard to throw away even the smallest piece of oak or the slimmest sliver of rosewood. After all, you just never know! This module allows you to keep lots of scrap neatly hidden, and there's plenty of room in the two drawers for miscellaneous tools and other shop paraphernalia.

Start by building the carcass and face frame as described on page 83, then add the horizontal divider (A) and its corresponding face-frame piece (B). Rip, then crosscut the drawer pieces (C, D, E, F) to size. Using the same drawer assembly as that on pages 83 and 84, put together the two drawers. (Cut three pieces of F—you'll need one piece for the bottom of the scrap bin.)

Cut the scrap-bin pieces (F, G, H, I) to size. Using a sabersaw, cut the drawer-front opening to size. The large opening is great for tossing in scrap pieces without having to stop and pull open a drawer. If you don't need scrap storage, eliminate the opening and add a drawer pull. Cut the rabbets in the bin-door front and at the back of each drawer side. Also cut the grooves in the front and sides. Glue and clamp the bin together.

Mask the pine parts and paint the rest as shown in the photo, *right*. Remove the tape; after the paint has dried, finish the pine trim with polyurethane. Attach the drawer slides and drawer pulls. *continued*

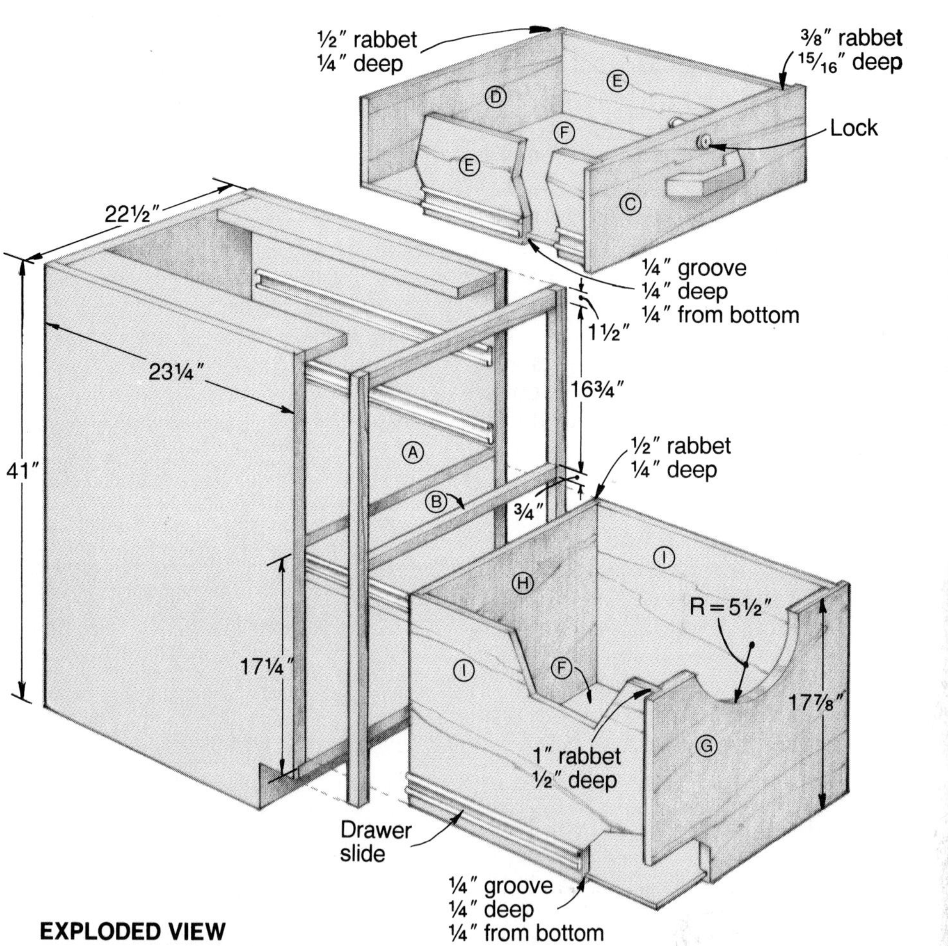

½″ rabbet
¼″ deep
⅜″ rabbet
15/16″ deep
Lock
D
E
F
E
C
22½″
23¼″
¼″ groove
¼″ deep
¼″ from bottom
1½″
16¾″
41″
A
B
¾″
½″ rabbet
¼″ deep
I
H
R = 5½″
17¼″
I
F
1″ rabbet
½″ deep
G
17⅞″
Drawer
slide
¼″ groove
¼″ deep
¼″ from bottom

EXPLODED VIEW

Bill of Materials

Part	Finished Size T	W	L	Mat.	Qty.
A divider	¾″	22⅛″	22½″	PLY	1
B face frame	¾″	¾″	22½″	P	1
C drawer front	¾″	8¼″	22⅜″	PLY	2
D drawer back	½″	7¾″	21″	PLY	2
E drawer side	½″	8¼″	22⅝″	PLY	4
F drwr./bin bottom	¼″	21″	22½″	HB	3
G bin front	¾″	17⅞″	22⅜″	PLY	1
H bin back	½″	16½″	21 1/16″	PLY	1
I bin side	½″	17″	22⅝″	PLY	2

Material Key: PLY—plywood, P—pine, HB—hardboard.
Supplies: polyurethane finish, 3 pairs—22″ drawer slides, 2—wood pulls, 2—locks, paint.

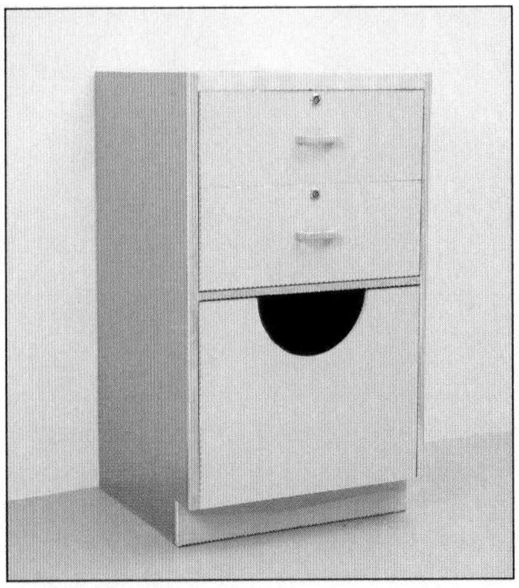

Scrap bin/storage unit

MODULAR WORKBENCH GROUP
continued

Drawer Bridge and Roll-Around Cabinet

Go to where the action is with this winning combo. The tool totes pull out, and the roll-around unit slides out of its cubbyhole for help where you need it.

Construct the bridge-unit carcass (A, B, C, D) by ripping and crosscutting the pieces to size, then assembling. Cut the face-frame pieces (E, F, G, H) to size, then glue and nail them to the bridge unit. Cut and assemble the tool-tray drawers (I, J, K, L). (Use the drawer-assembly instructions on pages 83 and 84 and the dimensions given in the Bill of Materials at *right*.)

To build the roll-around, cut the carcass pieces (M, N, O, P, Q) and frame pieces (R, S, T) to size, then assemble. Add the lip (U, V) to the top of the unit. Cut the

doors (W) to size and attach. Finally, cut the drawer parts (X, Y, Z, AA) to size and assemble.

Mask the pine pieces with tape, and paint the rest. Remove the tape and, after the paint dries, finish the pine with oil or polyurethane. Attach the casters to the roll-around, and screw the bridge unit between two adjacent cabinets.

Drawer bridge/cabinet

Bill of Materials

Part	Finished Size			Mat.	Qty.
	T	W	L		
Drawer Unit					
A bridge top	¾"	22½"	22½"	PLY	2
B bridge side	¾"	8¼"	23¼"	PLY	2
C bridge divider	¾"	6¾"	22½"	PLY	1
D bridge back	¾"	8¼"	22½"	PLY	1
E face frame	¾"	¾"	22½"	P	1
F face frame	¾"	¾"	8¼"	P	2
G face frame	¾"	¾"	6"	P	1
H face frame	¾"	1½"	22½"	P	1
I tray side	½"	5⅞"	22⅞"	PLY	4
J tray back	¾"	5⅞"	10¼"	PLY	2
K tray bottom	¼"	10¼"	22¼"	HB	2
L tray front	¾"	5⅞"	10¾"	PLY	2
Roll-Around Cabinet					
M top	¾"	22"	22½"	PLY	1
N side	¾"	23¼"	31¼"	PLY	2
O bottom	¾"	22⅞"	22¾"	PLY	1
P back	¾"	22"	31¼"	PLY	1
Q rail	¾"	2"	22"	PLY	1
R face frame	¾"	4¼"	23½"	P	1
S face frame	¾"	¾"	22"	P	1
T face frame	¾"	¾"	27"	P	2
U lip	¾"	1"	23½"	P	2
V lip	¾"	1"	24"	P	2
W door	¾"	10⅞"	23"	PLY	2
X drawer front	¾"	3"	21⅞"	PLY	1
Y drawer back	½"	2½"	20⅝"	PLY	1
Z drawer side	½"	3"	22⅝"	PLY	2
AA drawer bottom	¼"	20⅝"	22¼"	HB	1

Material Key: PLY—plywood, P—pine, HB—hardboard.
Supplies: Paint, 1 pair—22" drawer slides, 5—wood pulls, 4—2" wraparound hinges, polyurethane, 2—¾ × 21⅜" dowels, lock and catch, 2—4" swivel casters, 2—4" fixed casters.

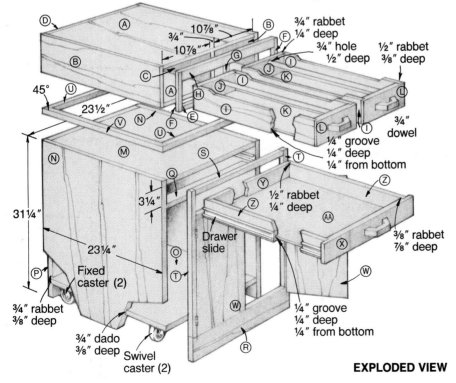

EXPLODED VIEW

Drill-Press Stand

This drill-press stand measures 38" high, 19¾" deep, and 15" wide. If you prefer a different height, change the width of pedestal pieces O and P.

To construct the stand, assemble the cabinet carcass (A–F) as shown at *right*. Use dowel joints to build the face frame (G–I). Glue and nail the face frame to the cabinet. Build and fit the door (J) and drawer (K–N).

Construct the pedestal (O, P) and top (Q–S). Countersink and screw the top to the pedestal and the pedestal to the cabinet. Cover the top with laminate. Use carriage bolts to bolt your drill press through the top (Q) and through the cabinet top (A) for a sturdy support. Paint, let dry, and attach pulls and hardware.

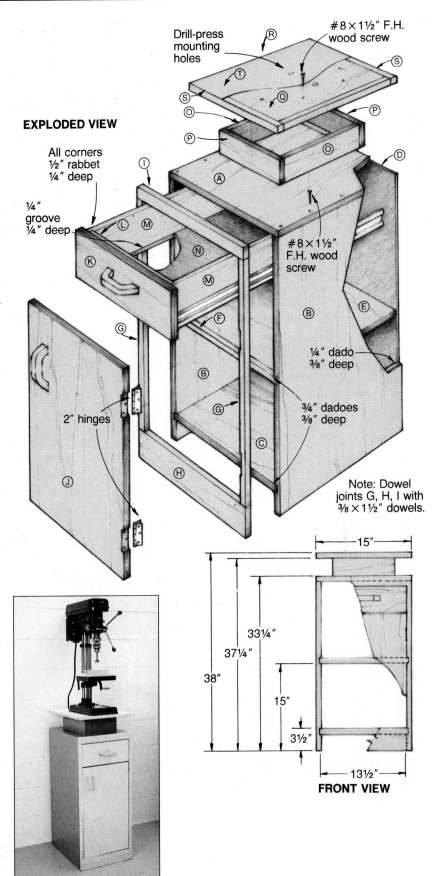

EXPLODED VIEW

Drill-press mounting holes

#8×1½" F.H. wood screw

All corners ½" rabbet ¼" deep

¼" groove ¼" deep

#8×1½" F.H. wood screw

2" hinges

¼" dado ⅜" deep

¾" dadoes ⅜" deep

Note: Dowel joints G, H, I with ⅜ × 1½" dowels.

Drill-press stand

FRONT VIEW

15"
33¼"
37¼"
38"
15"
3½"
13½"

Bill of Materials

Part	Finished Size			Mat.	Qty.
	T	W	L		
A top	¾"	15"	19"	PLY	1
B side	¾"	19"	32½"	PLY	2
C bottom	¾"	18¾"	14¼"	PLY	1
D back	¼"	14¼"	32⅞"	HB	1
E shelf	¾"	18"	14¼"	PLY	1
F edge	¾"	¾"	14¼"	P	1
G frame	¾"	¾"	28¾"	P	2
H frame	¾"	3"	15"	P	1
I frame	¾"	1½"	15"	P	1
J door	¾"	13⅜"	23"	PLY	1
K drawer front	¾"	5½"	13⅜"	PLY	1
L drawer front	½"	5½"	12"	P	2
M drawer side	½"	5½"	18"	P	2
N drawer bottom	¼"	12"	17½"	HB	1
O pedestal	¾"	4"	12¼"	PLY	2
P pedestal	¾"	4"	9"	PLY	2
Q top	¾"	13½"	18¼"	PLY	1
R edging	¾"	¾"	18¼"	P	2
S edging	¾"	¾"	15"	P	2

Material Key: PLY—plywood, HB—hardboard, P—pine.
Supplies: 2—18" drawer slides, 2—2" butt hinges, 1 door catch, 2—hardwood pulls, #8×1½" flathead wood screws, 6d finish nails, contact cement, polyurethane, paint, 4—⅜ × 1½" dowels, plastic laminate.

TRIPLE-CROWN SAWHORSE

This handy-to-have-around sawhorse literally rises to the occasion. Build one for use as a ripping support, or build a pair and raise projects to back-pleasing heights.

Form the end supports

1. Cut two pieces of ¾" plywood (we used A–C fir plywood) to 20 × 22¾" for the end supports (A).

2. Cut two pieces of ¾" maple to ¾" wide by 20" long for the banding (B). Glue one piece to the bottom of each end support.

3. Using the dimensions on the Exploded View Drawing, *opposite,* mark a centerline the length of one end support. Measuring from the centerline, lay out and cut the angled sides on one end support. Use this support as a template to mark the shape onto the second end support, then cut it to shape.

4. From the centerpoint at the bottom, mark a 4" radius. Cut the arc to shape, and again use this support as a template to mark the arc onto the second support. Cut the second support to shape, and sand both arcs smooth.

Attach the center panels to the end supports

1. Cut the spacers (C) to size. Center the spacers on each end support, and glue and screw them into place, using the hole sizes in the Screw Hole Detail, *opposite.*

2. Cut the two center panels (D) to size. Locate and mark the center of one panel, and mark a 14"-diameter circle. Drill a blade-start hole, cut the circle to shape with a jigsaw, and sand smooth. (The circle cutting helps reduce the total weight of the sawhorse.) Trace the circle outline onto the second panel, and cut that circle to shape.

3. On one center panel, mark the locations for the two ⅜"

holes, referring to the Exploded View Drawing for dimensions. Clamp the two panels together with the edges flush, and drill ⅜" holes through both panels where marked. Remove the clamps.

4. Cut the four maple corner braces (E) to size, bevel-ripping a chamfer along one edge of each.

5. With the top edges flush, glue and screw one center panel (D) to a spacer (C) on each end support (A). See the Screw Hole Detail for hole sizes. Repeat for the second panel. Now glue and screw the four corner braces (E) into position.

Add the adjustable center support

1. Cut the adjustable support (F) to 19 × 29". Mark and cut a taper on each end of the piece

(see the Exploded View Drawing for dimensions).

2. Cut the top beam (G) to size (we cut ours from a 2 × 4). Rout a ¼" round-over along the top edges of the beam. Cut or rout a ¾" groove ¾" deep down the center of the beam. Center and glue the beam to the top of the adjustable support.

3. Slide the adjustable support between the center panels. Using the two previously drilled ⅜" holes in the panels as guides, drill just far enough into the adjustable support to make a mark in it.

4. Remove the support, and drill a pair of ¾" holes through the support where marked with the ⅜" bit. Now, as shown in the

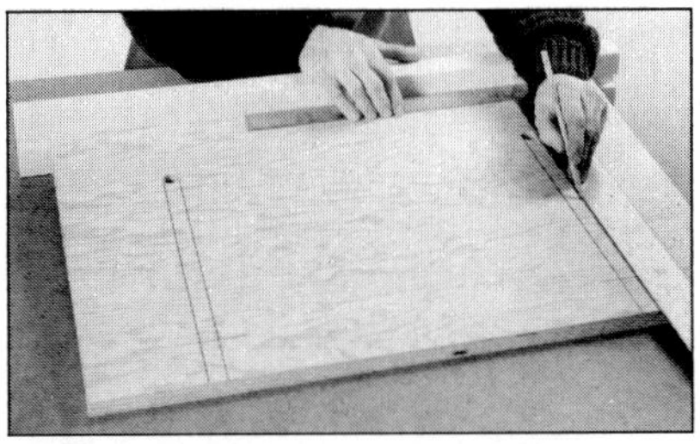

Mark lines on the adjustable support, perpendicular to the beam, on each side of the holes.

photo *above,* mark parallel lines on each side of each ¾″ hole to the bottom of the support. Center and bore a ¾″ hole between the lines 2″ from the bottom of the support where shown on the Exploded View Drawing.

5. Using a jigsaw, saw along the marked lines from hole to hole to form the 12¾″-long slots where shown on the Exploded View Drawing.

6. Slide the support between the center panels until the top beam rests on top of the center panel, and trace the 14″-diameter circle onto the support. Remove the support, and cut out the hole.

Make the wrench and add the carriage bolts

1. To make the wrench (H) to be used for ease in loosening and tightening the wing nuts, cut a piece of ¾″ maple to 1¼×3″. Using tracing paper, transfer the Wing Nut Wrench Pattern at *right* onto the stock. Drill the holes where shown and cut the wrench to shape.

2. Sand the parts smooth, and prime and paint as desired.

3. Position the adjustable support between center panels. Install carriage bolts through holes. Slide a flat washer onto each bolt, then thread on wing nuts. Drill a 5⁄32″ pilot hole ½″ deep, and add a #8×1¼″ screw to hang the wrench.

4. Raise the adjustable support to the desired height, and use the wrench to tighten the wing nuts.

If you have an uneven shop floor, the tapered sides on the adjustable support allow the support to be tilted and positioned level.

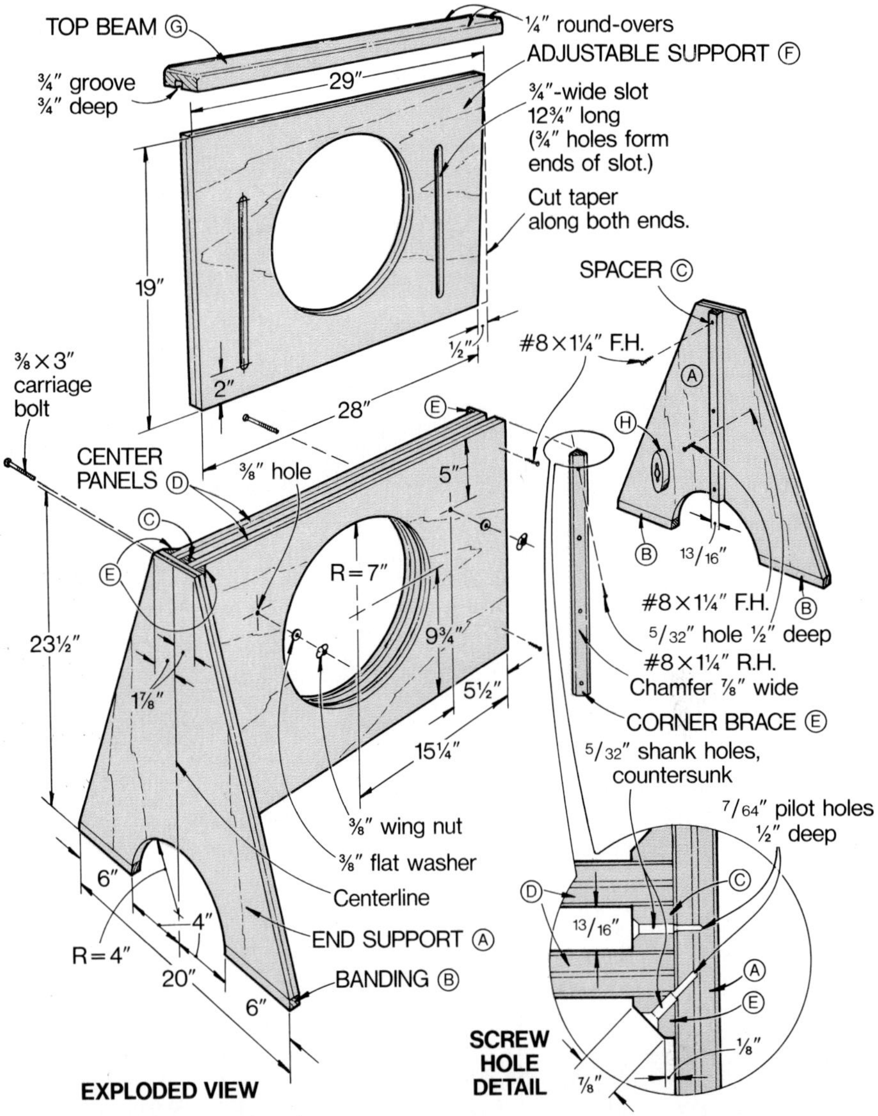

TOP BEAM G
¼″ round-overs
ADJUSTABLE SUPPORT F
¾″ groove
¾″ deep
29″
¾″-wide slot
12¾″ long
(¾″ holes form
ends of slot.)
Cut taper
along both ends.
19″
SPACER C
½″
#8×1¼″ F.H.
⅜×3″
carriage
bolt
2″
28″
E
A
H
CENTER
PANELS D
⅜″ hole
5″
C
E
R=7″
B
13/16″
#8×1¼″ F.H.
B
5/32″ hole ½″ deep
#8×1¼″ R.H.
Chamfer ⅞″ wide
23½″
1⅞″
9¾″
5½″
CORNER BRACE E
15¼″
5/32″ shank holes,
countersunk
⅜″ wing nut
7/64″ pilot holes
½″ deep
⅜″ flat washer
Centerline
D
C
6″
13/16″
4″
END SUPPORT A
R=4″
A
20″
BANDING B
E
6″
SCREW
HOLE
DETAIL
⅛″
⅞″
EXPLODED VIEW

WING NUT WRENCH (H)

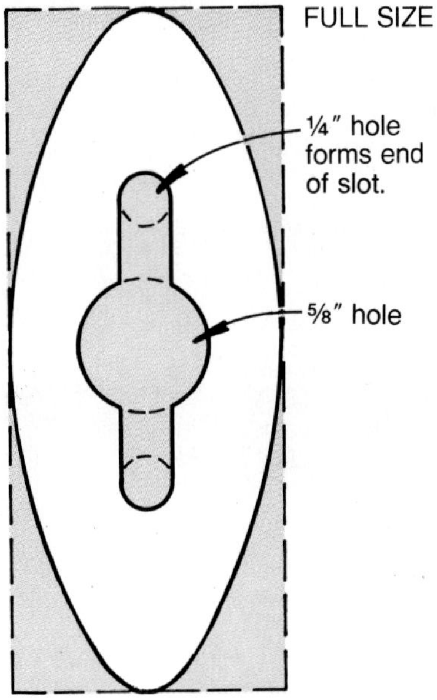

FULL SIZE
¼″ hole
forms end
of slot.
⅝″ hole

Bill of Materials					
Part	Finished Size*			Mat.	Qty.
	T	W	L		
A* support	¾″	20″	22¾″	PLY	2
B* banding	¾″	¾″	6″	M	4
C spacer	¾″	13⁄16″	19½″	M	2
D panel	¾″	19½″	30½″	PLY	2
E brace	¾″	¾″	19½″	M	4
F* adjust. support	¾″	19″	29″	PLY	1
G beam	1½″	3½″	34″	P/F	1
H* wrench	¾″	1¼″	3″	M	1

*Parts marked with an * are cut larger initially, then trimmed to finished size. Please read the instructions before cutting.

Material Key: PLY—plywood, M—maple, P/F—pine or fir.
Supplies: #8×1¼″ F.H. wood screws, #8×1¼″ R.H. wood screw, 2—⅜×3″ carriage bolts with flat washers and wing nuts, primer, paint.

STORAGE FOR SANDING

Keep sheets of varying grits within easy reach in one of these handy units. The bin at *left* has angled shelves and a paper-tearing device for less fumbling and faster finishing. The one *below* stores everything you need—sanders, sandpaper, and sanding belts—in a convenient, wall-hung cabinet.

Sandpaper storage bin (opposite)

Sander/sandpaper cabinet (page 94)

Bill of Materials					
Part	**Finished Size**			**Mat.**	**Qty.**
	T	**W**	**L**		
A side	¾″	10″	13¼″	PLY	2
B top/ bottom	¾″	10″	12¼″	PLY	2
C shelf	⅛″	10″	12³⁄₁₆″	HB	7
D back	⅛″	13″	13¼″	HB	1
E facing strip	¼″	¾″	13¼″	B	2
F facing strip	¼″	¾″	13″	B	2
G tearing guide	¼″	¾″	10″	B	2

Material Key: PLY—plywood, HB—hardboard, B—birch.
Supplies: #4×½″ panhead screws, #8×¾″ roundhead brass wood screws, ½″ brads, 2—10⅜″ hacksaw blades, paint, oil finish, wood putty.

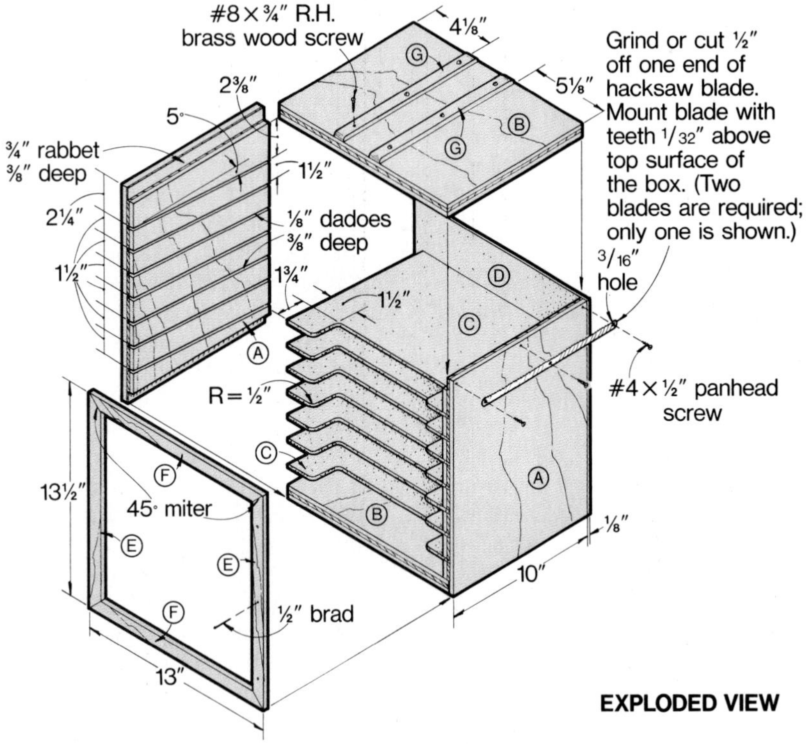
#8×¾″ R.H.
brass wood screw
4⅛″
5⅛″
Grind or cut ½″ off one end of hacksaw blade. Mount blade with teeth 1/32″ above top surface of the box. (Two blades are required; only one is shown.)
2⅜″
5°
¾″ rabbet
⅜″ deep
1½″
2¼″
⅛″ dadoes
⅜″ deep
1½″
1¾″
1½″
3/16″
hole
R=½″
#4×½″ panhead
screw
13½″
45° miter
⅛″
10″
½″ brad
13″
A
B
C
D
E
F
G

EXPLODED VIEW

Sandpaper Storage Bin

Hacksaw blades on the upper corners of this handy cabinet let you cut sandpaper down to size in a jiffy.

1. To build the box, cut the plywood frame parts (A, B), the hardboard shelves (C), and the hardboard back (D) to the sizes indicated in the Bill of Materials. Mark and cut the cutouts in the front of each shelf, rounding the corners where shown on the Exploded View Drawing, *above right*.

2. Measure, mark, and cut the dadoes and rabbets in the sides (A) where dimensioned in the drawing. (To cut the dadoes for the shelves, we first aligned our radial-arm saw blade with the 5°-angled lines that we had just marked. To dado the left side, angle the blade left of center, and to cut the right side, angle the blade right of center. You could cut the dadoes on your tablesaw with a miter gauge fitted with an auxiliary fence.) Glue, clamp, and nail the box assembly together.

3. Sand the box. Then paint or finish it to match your shop cabinets.

4. Miter-cut the facing strips (E, F) to length, finish-sand, and attach them to the box with glue and brads. Set the brads and fill the holes.

5. To make the paper-tearing device, first grind the two hacksaw blades to 10″ in length. Then drill a ³⁄₁₆″ hole in the ground end and one in the center of each blade (the blade comes with the third hole predrilled). Drill pilot holes and screw a blade to each side of the box.

6. Cut the tearing guides (G) to size, finish-sand, and attach them to the top of the box where indicated. (The *right* guide is 5½″ from the right edge of the box, and the *left* guide is 4½″ from the left edge.) When the guides are mounted where shown, you can halve and quarter a standard sheet of sandpaper to fit most palm-grip sanders. Apply an oil finish to the facing strips.

Tearing sandpaper to size

Position a full sheet of sandpaper with the short (9″) side against the right-hand guide. Holding the piece firmly against the guide, slowly tear the paper by pulling it down across the hacksaw blade. Now position the resulting half with the short side against the left-hand guide and tear it in half on the other blade. *continued*

STORAGE FOR SANDING
continued

Sander/Sandpaper Cabinet

Here's another way to ensure that you'll spend less time gritting your teeth and more time sanding. Besides sandpaper, this convenient cabinet also accommodates a portable belt sander and a palm-grip sander.

1. From a sheet of ¾" particleboard, lay out and cut parts A through I to finished size. (We cut E and F to size plus 2" in length to allow for ease in bevel-cutting these pieces later.)

2. Bevel-cut the front end of the shelves for the two sanders (E, F) to a 60° angle; cut the back end to a 30° angle. Cut dadoes in the shelf dividers (D) and inside the right-hand side (C) where shown on the Exploded View Drawing, *below.*

3. Glue and screw the back (A), bottom (B), and sides (C)

together. Then glue and screw the cleats (J, K) and the slanted shelves (E, F) in position. Drill two holes in the back for screws or wall anchors, according to wall-stud spacing.

4. Loose-fit the shelf dividers (D) and shelves (G, H), starting with the left-hand divider and working toward the right-hand one. As you slide in the center and right-hand shelves (H), glue in the false back (I) for each shelf where shown on the drawing.

5. Glue and screw the top (B) on the cabinet. Sand all edges flush. Mask off the pine cleats, then paint all exposed surfaces to the desired color. Cut the pine trim strips (L, M, N, O) to finished size. Finish all the pine pieces with polyurethane or other clear finish. Attach the trim strips to the cabinet face. Attach cup hooks for electrical cords. Hang the cabinet.

Bill of Materials

Part	Finished Size*			Mat.	Qty.
	T	W	L		
A back	¾"	13½"	23¾"	PB	1
B top/ bottom	¾"	12½"	23¾"	PB	2
C side	¾"	12½"	14¾"	PB	2
D divider	¾"	11¾"	13½"	PB	3
E* shelf	¾"	8"	12¾"	PB	1
F* shelf	¾"	5"	12¾"	PB	1
G shelf	¾"	3¾"	11¾"	PB	3
H shelf	¾"	5¼"	6¼"	PB	4
I false back	¾"	2¾"	5"	PB	5
J cleat	¾"	1¼"	5"	P	1
K cleat	¾"	1¼"	8"	P	1
L trim	¼"	¾"	13½"	P	5
M trim	¼"	¾"	25¼"	P	2
N trim	¼"	¾"	3½"	P	3
O trim	¼"	¾"	5"	P	4

*Cut these pieces extra long, then bevel-cut to final lengths.

Material Key: PB—particleboard, P—pine.
Supplies: #8 × 1¼" flathead wood screws, ½" brads, 2—1½" cup hooks, latex paint, wall anchors or screws for wall mounting.

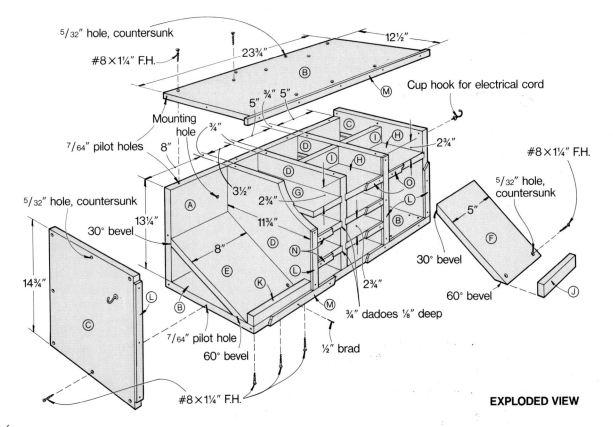

EXPLODED VIEW

DRUM-SANDER HOLDER

Tired of your sanding drums and sleeves rolling around your shop—or worse yet, not being able to find them? Solve the problem in a hurry with our wall-mounted holder. The drum shafts fit in holes in the top, and there's plenty of room below for the sanding drum sleeves.

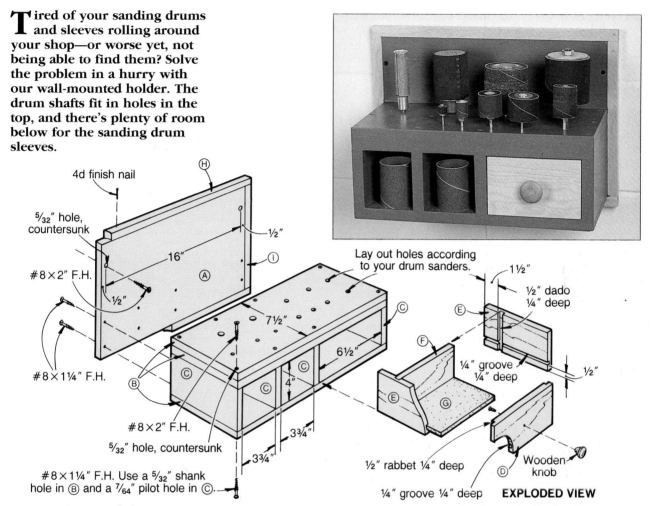

Lay out holes according to your drum sanders.

4d finish nail

$\frac{5}{32}$" hole, countersunk

16"

$\frac{1}{2}$"

#8 × 2" F.H.

$\frac{1}{2}$"

#8 × 1¼" F.H.

7½"

6½"

4"

#8 × 2" F.H.

$\frac{5}{32}$" hole, countersunk

3¾"

3¾"

#8 × 1¼" F.H. Use a $\frac{5}{32}$" shank hole in Ⓑ and a $\frac{7}{64}$" pilot hole in Ⓒ.

1½"

½" dado ¼" deep

¼" groove ¼" deep

½"

½" rabbet ¼" deep

Wooden knob

¼" groove ¼" deep   **EXPLODED VIEW**

1. Cut the back (A), storage box tops and bottom (B), and dividers (C) to size. Laminate the two top pieces. Lay out and drill 1"-deep holes in the top to house the shanks of your drum sanders.

2. Glue and clamp the storage box together. Drill shank and pilot holes, and drive the screws.

3. Cut the drawer front (D), sides (E), back (F), and bottom (G) to size. Cut or rout a ¼" groove ¼" deep ½" from the bottom in the drawer front and sides. Cut a ½" dado ¼" deep 1½" from the back edge of each drawer side. Then cut a ½" rabbet ¼" deep along both ends of the drawer front (D).

4. Glue and clamp the drawer together, checking for square.

Drill a hole through the drawer front and attach a knob.

5. Cut trim pieces (H, I) to size; glue and nail them to the back (A).

6. Glue and clamp the storage box to the back piece. Drill shank and pilot holes from the back side of the back piece into the back of the box, and screw the back to the box.

7. Mask off the trim pieces and paint the storage box and back. Remove the masking tape and apply a clear finish to the trim and drawer.

8. Drill the mounting holes through the back piece, and fasten the holder securely to your shop wall.

Bill of Materials

Part	Finished Size			Mat.	Qty.
	T	W	L		
A back	¾"	11"	17"	PB	1
B bottom	¾"	7½"	17"	PB	3
C divider	¾"	4"	7½"	PB	4
D drawer front	½"	3$\frac{15}{16}$"	6$\frac{7}{16}$"	P	1
E drwr. side	½"	3$\frac{15}{16}$"	7¼"	P	2
F drwr. back	½"	3$\frac{3}{16}$"	5$\frac{15}{16}$"	P	1
G drawer bottom	¼"	5$\frac{15}{16}$"	7¼"	HB	1
H trim	¾"	¾"	18½"	P	2
I trim	¾"	¾"	11"	P	2

Material Key: PB—particleboard, P—pine, HB—hardboard.

Supplies: #8 × 1¼" flathead wood screws, #8 × 2" flathead wood screws, wooden knob, 4d finish nails, masking tape, paint.

ACKNOWLEDGMENTS

Project Designers

Dave Ashe—Modular Workbench Group, pages 82–89

Marvin Barsness—Fine-Finish Scraper, pages 14–15

Jim Boelling—Pocket-Size Try Square, pages 8–10; Fine-Finish Scraper, pages 14–15; Hard Maple Woodworker's Mallets, pages 22–23; Double-Duty Tablesaw Extensions, pages 32–35; Benchtop Router Table, pages 38–40; Plane Rack, page 81; Triple-Crown Sawhorse, pages 90–91

Larry Clayton—Walnut-Maple Miter Box, pages 24–25

James R. Downing—Handscrew Clamps, pages 5–7; Strip Sander, pages 11–13; Depth Gauge, pages 16–17; Marking Gauge, pages 20–21; Easy-to-Adjust Rip Fence, pages 27–31; Heavy-Duty Router Table, pages 41–47; Delta-Wing Pin-Routing Attachment, pages 48–50; Back-to-Basics Shop Lathe, pages 54–63; Triple-Crown Sawhorse, pages 90–91

Kim Downing—One-Weekend Workbench, pages 75–80

Randall Foshee—Double-Duty Tablesaw Extensions, pages 32–35

Gary Hood—Drum-Sanding Table, pages 64–66

Marlen Kemmet—Sandpaper Storage Bin, page 93

Bill Lovelace—Drum-Sander Holder, page 95

Paul L. McClure—Blade-Height Gauge, pages 36–37

Don Mostrom—Thickness Sander, pages 67–73

M. C. "Morrie" Patten—Sanding Block, pages 18–19

Wilbur Rath—Accurate Box-Joint Jig, pages 51–53

Photographers

Craig Anderson
Bob Calmer
George Ceolla
Hopkins Associates
Jim Kascoutas
Scott Little

Illustrators

Ron Chamberlain
James R. Downing
Kim Downing
Randall Foshee
Mike Henry
Bill Zaun